# SHADOW LIFE

# SHADOW LIFE

## A Portrait of Anne Frank and Her Family

### BARRY DENENBERG

Hodder
Children's
Books

A division of Hodder Headline Limited

ACKNOWLEDGMENTS

My deepest thanks to David Caplan, Amy Griffin, Sheila Keenan, John
Marchesella, Terra McVoy, Arlene Robillard, Mark Seidenfeld, Liz Szabla,
and everyone at Scholastic who worked so hard on *Shadow Life*.

PHOTO CREDITS

Hulton / Getty

Anne Frank Fonds-Basel / Anne Frank House

ISBN-10: 0340917121
ISBN-13: 9780340917121

Printed and bound in Great Britain by
Bookmarque Ltd, Croydon, Surrey

The paper and board used in this paperback by Hodder Children's Books are natural
recyclable products made from wood grown in sustainable forests. The manufacturing
processes conform to the environmental regulations of the country of origin.

Hodder Children's Books
a division of Hodder Headline Limited
338 Euston Road
London NW1 3BH

*TO MY FAMILY*

# CONTENTS

# INTRODUCTION

I FIRST READ *Anne Frank: The Diary of a Young Girl* (I was ashamed to realise) in 1994. At first Anne's diary annoyed me: it was fragmented, unstructured, unedited, and unrelentingly precocious and self-absorbed. But it was also unashamedly introspective and unselfconsciously intimate. Fortunately it dawned on me that this was exactly what the diary of an intelligent thirteen-year-old girl with the talent and inclination to record her thoughts and experiences would sound like.

Three years later, in 1997, I read a provocative and what turned out to be inspirational article in the *New Yorker*: Cynthia Ozick's "Who Owns Anne Frank?" It caused me to question my understanding of the diary and subsequently the way the Holocaust is presented to young readers.

Although I am Jewish and throughout my life had read about World War II and the Holocaust, Ozick's article showed me how truly ignorant I was on the subject. I read all the books mentioned in it and watched Jon Blair's Academy Award–winning documentary *Anne Frank Remembered* — a further inspiration.

I decided that my next project would be a compelling and complete portrait of Anne Frank, her family, and the times they lived in. Five years later, when my research, note-taking, and organisation of materials was complete, I began to contemplate the structure of *Shadow Life*.

I wanted to make the first part of Anne Frank's life, in prewar Frankfurt and Amsterdam, as rich, detailed, and alive as possible. That section, I thought, would be best told in a conventional, narrative fashion.

But the second part, the family's two years in hiding, could not. I didn't want to simply recapitulate what Anne had written, but illuminate it. I was unsure of the right way to approach it and reread Anne's diary, hoping for a sign.

It was there.

On Friday, October 16, 1942, Anne wrote:

*Margot and I got into the same bed together last evening;*
*it was a frightful squash, but that was just the fun of it.*
*She asked if she could read my diary. I said, "Yes — at*
*least bits of it"; and then I asked her if I could read hers.*

Margot, Anne's introspective, self-effacing older sister, must have also kept a diary during their time in hiding (and possibly before). As if to accentuate the miracle of Anne's diary surviving, Margot's — like so many others — must have disappeared in the chaos and destruction of the war.

Imagining and re-creating Margot Frank's diary was an undertaking that could not be passed up, because it allowed me to accomplish so many important things:

≡ The everyday matters of the family's years in hiding could be described without being redundant for those who had already read the diary or wished to after reading *Shadow Life*.

≡ The reader could get a different perspective on Anne — what better source than her older sister? — and her intense relationship with her family.

≡ The personalities and dynamics of the other people in hiding could be seen through a lens different from Anne's.

≡ Readers could learn something of Margot, like Anne, a teenager forced to witness the world she loved disintegrate.

≡ Margot's highly regarded intelligence and political interests could be a valid vehicle for conveying what was happening historically in both the Netherlands and the world.

≡ Writing as Margot would allow me to confront one of, if not *the,* critical issue raised by Cynthia Ozick: Anne and her family's Jewishness. Unlike her irreligious father and free-spirited sister, Margot was, like her mother, a practising Jew as well as an earnest young Zionist who dreamed of someday immigrating to what is today Israel and becoming a midwife.

Biographers of Anne Frank understandably use Margot only to more fully realise their picture of Anne. As in life, Margot is not the focus of attention, Anne is. But fortunately there is some historical information available and several revealing letters written by Margot to a pen pal in Iowa, which Anne had preserved in her diary. These letters reveal that Margot was pragmatic, affectless, and wise beyond her years. It is almost as if childhood and her teenage years were something Margot couldn't be bothered with. These letters gave me valuable additional insight into her personality and provided the parameters of how she would speak and write. I developed an intricate profile of Margot, which I kept beside me along with her letters while imagining her diary.

But my problems weren't over. The third part of *Shadow Life* presented yet another challenge.

Early in my research, I came to have a much better understanding of why Ozick — and so many others writing about the Holocaust — believed ". . . the diary itself, richly crammed though it is with incident and passion, cannot count as Anne Frank's story. A story may not be said to be a story if the end is missing."

How was I to present the "end" — the last seven months of Anne Frank's life — in a way that was historically accurate and would truly speak to my audience?

I found my answer in *Voices from Vietnam,* which I had written ten years earlier. The book originally combined my historical narrative with first-person accounts of the men and women who had served in the Vietnam War. After three years of research and writing, however, something was not right. Getting it right had become a frustrating, daily struggle. Early one morning, I decided to remove nearly 80 per cent of my writing (leaving just enough narrative to provide the necessary chronology and historical background) so that the "voices" could come through loud and clear.

By relying on first-person narratives for Part Three of *Shadow Life,* I hoped the voices of the survivors of Westerbork, Auschwitz and Bergen-Belsen would also come through. Part Three is constructed as an oral history by the people who were in those same concentration camps, many at the same time as and alongside Anne and her family — some up until the end.

Ozick rightly takes issue with a line taken out of context from Anne's diary, the one that concludes the 1955 play and the 1959 movie: ". . . in spite of everything I still believe that people are really good at heart."

Of course, no one familiar with Anne Frank's last days would think she continued to feel this way. But tragically this same misleading line, erroneously implying that there is something uplifting in Anne's brief life and unspeakably horrific death, is still being used today as part of the Holocaust curriculum for many secondary school students.

Recent historical scholarship meant for adult readers has been providing newly conceived and researched analysis as well as valuable accounts of the Holocaust that are important additions to the already vast literature. This same evolution in thought and writing on the subject should be made available to young readers. It is time to reintroduce the story of Anne Frank to a new generation.

As I write this, we are approaching what would be Anne Frank's seventy-fifth birthday. February–March 2005 will mark the sixtieth anniversary of her death.

We live at a time when insensitivity to the value of human life is on the rise; reading about Anne Frank is, it seems to me, especially urgent and meaningful now.

If there is any hope it lies within us.

Perhaps we will finally understand that the object of hate, violence, and evil may be a child just like ourselves. Perhaps even a young girl living in Amsterdam who has just celebrated her thirteenth birthday and has joyously received the only gift she cared about — a diary. Someone with her whole life before her . . .

Maybe if we realise that each life is precious, then the diary that Anne was given can be a gift to us, too.

BARRY DENENBERG

MAY 2004

# PART ONE

# LIVING

# Frankfurt, Germany

≡ 1933 ≡

In 1932, the National Socialist German Workers' Party, its members known as Nazis (*NA*tionalso*ZI*alistische), was democratically elected (polling fourteen million votes) to preside over the government. The head of the party, forty-three-year-old Austrian-born Adolf Hitler, was appointed chancellor in January 1933.

The election took place three years after the New York Stock Exchange crashed, triggering a worldwide economic depression. In Germany, unemployment was at an all-time high — directly and tragically affecting thirteen million people, if spouses and children were considered. Men walked the streets wearing signs asking for jobs, any jobs. It was estimated that nearly half a million people were homeless. The result of all this was deplorable living conditions for many German citizens.

Added to this were the financial payments Germany had to make to the countries that were victorious in the First World War, a provision of the Treaty of Versailles, which had ended that war. The overwhelming majority of the German population considered these payments harsh and humiliating, and even more punitive and unfair when combined with the current, severe economic crisis.

There was widespread unrest and an atmosphere of desperation. Germans rightly feared for their future and sought reasons for their plight and an end to their misery.

Adolf Hitler offered both.

According to Hitler there were two reasons for Germany's problems: the punishing stipulations of the Treaty of Versailles and the Jews. Although the Jewish people constituted less than one per cent of the population, Hitler and an increasing number of German citizens claimed they accounted for 100 per cent of the country's problems.

Adolf Hitler proclaimed and preached the racial superiority of the German people. Germans were stronger, smarter, and better than other races. Their destiny was to dominate the earth. Maintaining the racial purity of the German people was essential, he said. He promised to make Germany Europe's most powerful country once again. He promised to take over adjoining land that rightfully belonged to

Germany, providing the "living space" they needed to prosper and thrive.

He was addressing an audience that was becoming increasingly militaristic, racist, and anti-Jewish.

To celebrate their victory at the polls, an estimated two million Nazi followers unleashed a nationwide campaign of intimidation and terror aimed at their opponents and all Jews.

Jewish writers, film directors, conductors and composers, philosophers, psychiatrists, and scientists (eventually including Albert Einstein) were forced to leave Germany.

In towns and cities across Germany, students who embraced the new Fascist philosophy took books that were written by Jews or were otherwise unacceptable from the libraries and burned them. These book burnings appeared spontaneous but were directed by Nazi Party officials who provided the lists of which books were to be destroyed.

The Nazi Party declared a boycott of Jewish-owned businesses: anti-Jewish slogans were painted on shop windows and signs were put up warning people not to shop there. Guards were posted outside to ensure that anyone who would have chosen to ignore the boycott was not allowed to.

Hundreds of thousands of people were arrested, supposedly

for political crimes, and hundreds and hundreds of others were kidnapped, beaten, tortured, and killed, all while the police stood by and did nothing. Gangs of "Brownshirts" (as Nazi followers were called because of the colour of their uniforms) roamed the streets of German cities looking for victims and shouting "Down with the Jews".

Otto and Edith Frank and their two daughters, Margot Betti (born February 16, 1926) and Annelies Marie (born June 12, 1929), were German Jews living in Frankfurt.

In 1925, thirty-six-year-old Otto, who had grown up in Frankfurt, married twenty-five-year-old Edith Holländer. Otto was charming, cultured, intelligent, and shrewd. He had gone to the university for a year and then travelled. At one point he lived in New York City, working in Macy's Department Store, which was owned by his classmate's relatives. He had the makings of the salesman and business-man he was to become. In the First World War he served as a German officer.

Edith came from a wealthy family and her large dowry was a factor for practical Otto, whose family fortunes had ebbed. Despite her youth she was somewhat old-fashioned, spoke only when she had something to say, and was courte-ous and thoughtful.

Neither was particularly religious, although Edith, unlike Otto, went to the synagogue. They observed some of the traditions of their religion, but not often and never strictly.

Like many Germans who were Jewish, they considered themselves Germans first: assimilated members of the population at large. Otto especially was a modern, liberal, progressive thinker, unbound by religious dogma. Reading, not religion, was sacred in the Frank household. Both Edith and Otto viewed the country of their birth as the most cultured and civilised place on earth.

That was about to change.

When they were first married they lived with Otto's mother and then, as economic and "other factors" dictated, they moved. Once they had to move because their landlord turned out to be a supporter of the Nazi Party's anti-Jewish views. No matter where they lived or how small or large their home, their main concern was that the children be happy and safe.

In the warmer months they played outside: Margot in the street with her many friends and Anne in the sandbox or large metal outdoor bath. When it snowed Margot towed her baby sister around on a sleigh.

Kathi, their trusted housekeeper, helped care for the

children, returning to help out even after she was married. Gertrude, a loving neighbour, was also like a member of the family.

Otto and Edith were glad their two daughters were growing up in a religiously diverse environment: their friends were Catholics, Protestants and Jews.

Otto was a particularly attentive and loving father. Most fathers of his time and place were solely concerned with obedience and proper behaviour (if they were concerned at all). "Pim", as he was called by his children (although no one knows why), would come home for lunch in the afternoons and play with and bathe his girls at night.

Margot was easy to care for. She slept through the night from the time she was born and never cried. She was a happy, contented child. Anne's difficult delivery was a harbinger of things to come. She had trouble breathing and let everyone know about it. She didn't sleep at night and cried out for days on end. Edith kept a baby book for both girls. Margot's went on at length, but Anne's was brief, to the point, and mostly medical.

Proper Edith took great pains with both girls' appearances. Their dresses were always freshly starched and ironed, their hair washed and combed. No matter how long or where Margot played she managed to remain that way. The "Little Princess", Kathi called her.

Once Anne, newly washed and dressed, was playing happily in a mud puddle when Kathi tried to remove her. Anne wanted Kathi to tell her a story first. Kathi said she didn't have time but Anne insisted it could be a *short* story.

Both girls delighted in hearing over and over again the tale, handed down from his mother to Otto, of the two Paulas. Good Paula and Bad Paula. Since they were invisible the only way to tell them apart was by their actions. Good Paula obeyed her parents, was nice to her sister, and finished everything on her plate. Bad Paula was, well, bad. She played with her food, annoyed insects and small animals, and was generally a trial. Predictably Margot clearly favoured Good Paula, while Anne was torn between the two.

Their happy home was, however, being threatened by the world outside their door. Otto and Edith saw the danger increasing with each passing day.

They sat in stony silence through dinners in which their companions suggested that Hitler should be given a chance. Perhaps he could improve the dire economic conditions. Equally troubling were discussions in which people made light of the situation. He'll go away, he won't last. Just wait it out, they said.

The Franks did not think Hitler was going to fade away. His anti-Jewish views were becoming alarmingly popular.

For most of their lives, religion had mattered little. Now there was something sinister about being Jewish. Now, because they were Jewish, friends and neighbours had become people to be feared.

The country where they were born and raised — the country that they loved — was disintegrating all around them, transforming itself into something they didn't recognise and where they were not welcome.

The writing was on the wall, but most didn't see it. Otto and Edith Frank did.

They would have to go. To stay was simply too risky.

Edith was heartbroken. They would have to pack up everything they owned and go to a strange, new country. And where would they go?

Otto favoured Amsterdam. He had travelled there frequently and had good business connections now. He liked the Dutch — they were a liberal and tolerant people who had remained neutral in the First World War.

Aachen, where Edith was born, was not far from Amsterdam. At least she and the girls could continue to visit her family.

In the summer of 1933, it was decided.

Thanks to some help from his relatives, Otto had lined up a job in Amsterdam. He would be working for Opekta, a Frankfurt-based company that manufactured pectin, the ingredient that made ground-up fruit turn to gel and, therefore, become jam or jelly. Otto would be establishing their Amsterdam branch.

Edith and the girls would stay with Edith's mother in Aachen while Otto went on ahead to Amsterdam, got settled in his new position, and found a nice place for them to live.

They would build a brand-new life there, far away from Hitler, Nazis, and their ideas of racial purity and racial hatred.

Margot was seven, Anne four.

# Amsterdam, Holland

≡ 1934–1939 ≡

Thoughtfully and methodically, as with everything he did, Otto Frank assembled his staff: Johannes Kleiman, a bookkeeper whom Otto had known for a number of years; Victor Kugler, Otto's right-hand man who supervised the staff and ran the office when Otto was out; full-time typist Bep Voskuijl; and Hermine Santrouschitz.

Hermine was born in Vienna, Austria. When the First World War ended, thousands of children were malnourished because of the scarcity of food. In desperation some of the children were sent to countries that had enough food. After the child regained his health he would be returned home. Eleven-year-old Hermine was sent to Holland, and became so close and comfortable with her new family that she never returned to Vienna. Her foster parents adopted her and gave her a Dutch nickname, Miep.

When Miep was hired, Otto Frank took her to the company kitchen. He gave her a recipe and the ingredients necessary for making jam: pectin, fruit, sugar, etc. Then he left. Miep's cooking thus far had been limited to making coffee, but she succeeded, and in the coming weeks, as Otto brought different fruits requiring different proportions, Miep always turned out delicious jam.

Now that she had acquired firsthand knowledge of the proper way to make jam, she could communicate this to the housewives who were Opekta's customers.

Soon Miep was doing just about anything: answering telephone inquiries from the housewives, helping with the book-keeping, and doing routine office work. Calm, confident, and dependable, she became Otto's executive secretary.

Progressive Otto put signs on trucks, created ads for newspapers, and made films to persuade housewives to make more jam.

Later, when they decided to diversify the business, he hired chain-smoking, fast-talking, joke-loving Hermann van Pels. He was an expert in spices, and his hypersensitive nose could distinguish and identify any herb. In the annexe behind the front office and warehouse building Otto built his private office and a staff kitchen. He left the second and third floors of the annexe unused.

They all worked well together. His employees appreciated the respectful and courteous way Otto treated them and repaid him with their best efforts and their loyalty. Otto worked longer hours in Amsterdam than he had in Frankfurt — most days he didn't come home until late. And his travelling forced him to be away for days at a time.

He found a third-floor apartment in a modern complex at 37 Merwedeplein, situated between wide, well-laid-out avenues in the same section of the city that Miep lived in. It was a perfect place to raise a family.

In December, Edith came with Margot and oversaw the delivery and unpacking of her fine, antique furniture. Anne stayed with her grandmother and uncles in Aachen. In February 1934, Anne was placed on the table in the new apartment in the middle of the other gifts as a special birthday present for her sister.

The Franks decided to send Anne to a Montessori school. The informally structured, ungraded school emphasised individual development and self-motivation rather than conformity and obedience. Pupils were not required to remain in their seats — they could walk around and even talk during class, which would suit the Franks' free-spirited younger daughter just fine.

Both girls could walk or ride their bikes to school.

Margot adjusted immediately to her new school and made friends easily. She read constantly and was consistently at the head of her class. (Although both parents respected the role of education they made it clear that good grades were not nearly as important as becoming a happy, healthy person.) Margot was turning out to be a studious (something emphasised by her spectacles), introspective, well-mannered girl more than willing to go unnoticed. Quite unlike her younger sister.

Anne liked her kindergarten where she immediately made friends with Hanneli "Lies" Goslar who, it turned out, lived right below the Franks. They met Suzanne "Sanne" Ledermann, who lived around the corner (but went to a different school), and the three became close friends. (Margot and Sanne's older sister, Barbara, became good friends also.) After a while the three of them were nearly inseparable, preferring to remain apart from the other, less sophisticated girls in the neighborhood.

The ongoing construction in the still-developing area provided them with the world's best playground, thanks to the piles of sand and construction material. (There was a "real" playground located in the middle of the complex.)

They wrote with chalk on the pavements, played marbles, hopscotch, hide-and-seek and tag. They rolled hoops, rode scooters, roller-skated, and in the winter skated on the ice. Anne, annoyed that she had to use her sister's old, out-of-fashion skates, pestered her parents until they bought her new ones, the kind with the blade already stitched to the shoe.

The girls did cartwheels and handstands, seeing how long they could remain on their hands, something Anne was not good at because of her double-jointed shoulder (which also prevented her from going to gym class). They performed plays in school and in various living rooms, which Anne *was* good at, and collected and traded picture postcards of movie stars and royalty. The girls passed around little autograph books, which were all the rage, in which they wrote their own poetry and added their own drawings.

They called one another via secret whistles, but no matter how much Anne tried to practise and how hard everyone tried to help she just couldn't learn to whistle. Endlessly inventive, when calling for her friends, Anne sang through the letter box.

Visiting Mr Frank's office was another favourite activity. They played secretary, placing urgent phone calls, paging one another on the intercom, and doing some important typing.

Summers and holidays they frequently holidayed together. They named one hotel they stayed at the Tomato House because of the vegetarian-only menu. They went to an amusement park and enjoyed their first visit to a house of mirrors. Anne learned to swim, which she became quite good at, bicycled in the countryside, and took the standard houseboat tours of some of the many Dutch canals.

Anne loved babies and couldn't stop herself from sneaking a peek beneath the covers of a passing pram. When Lies's baby sister was born, Anne loved to help take her for a stroll.

Lies and Anne were in the same class and sat next to each other most of the time. Anne, always a critical and demanding friend, thought Lies confided in her nervous and irritable mother too much and that she was a little too shy (but compared with Anne, anyone was).

Anne's invariably cheerful personality coupled with her mischievous mind made her endlessly fun to be with. Her irresistible and instinctual sense of humour bordered at times on the slapstick. She purposefully would move her double-jointed shoulder in and out of its socket, a sure crowd pleaser.

As they grew up together the three girls spent more and more time reading fashion magazines, gossiping about their favourite film stars, and discussing boys.

Anne was style conscious before any of her friends. When going to the dressmakers on Merwedeplein she knew just where she wanted the hemline of her dress and how big the shoulder pads should be. Vain and critical about herself, as she was about everyone around her, Anne thought her best feature was her hair. And that fiddling with it all the time was the best way to make sure it was still there.

Both daughters had health problems that concerned their parents. Margot had stomachaches too frequently, and Anne was frail with a possible heart condition. She had a recurring fever and would have to stay in bed, resting for days at a time, something easily-bored Anne truly hated. Her condition, however, seemed to improve as she grew.

Her mother was also concerned about things other than Anne's health. She appreciated Anne's talents as a comedian and was gratified and pleased by her close relationship with her grandmother and uncles. They were always greatly amused by her. Once, when she and her grandmother got on a crowded tram, five-year-old Anne asked aloud if anyone was going to offer their seat to this poor old lady.

But Edith wanted Anne to be more like Margot, to behave and listen when she was told to do something. Anne resented being compared with Margot, the model child, and it created some distance between them.

Edith disapproved of Anne's insistence on always being the centre of attention. Anne was too talkative, forcing

Margot to take a backseat all of the time. She was rebellious, impertinent, stubborn, and headstrong in the extreme.

Edith agreed with Ruth Goslar: "God knows everything, but Anne knows everything better."

Edith believed Anne was spoiled by her permissive and indulgent father. His daughter's boldness made him laugh (at least most of the time), and her sparkling personality was the only thing that took his mind off his worries. The two of them had a special and strong attachment, coupled with an exclusive verbal and nonverbal communication. They would take long walks together and make up stories. When Anne would spin out of control, not an infrequent occurrence, only Pim could calm her, just as he did when she was an infant. Only now instead of songs and soothing touches he whispered reminders about self-control. Anne's invariably positive response was fuelled by her intense drive to do anything to avoid displeasing her adored and devoted father.

She was truly a daddy's girl.

Edith and Anne clashed time and time again. From Anne's perspective her mother just wasn't the kind of woman she admired and, therefore, wasn't providing what Anne needed.

And Edith was having a difficult time of her own.

She resented being forced to leave Germany and was angry that she would never be able to return. She was perpetually homesick, enjoyed talking about the past, and had great difficulty adjusting to life in Holland. She did not make friends as easily as her sociable husband. He and the girls readily adapted to the customs of their new homeland. Margot and Anne soon considered themselves Dutch girls, no longer German. Unlike her daughters, who had effortlessly learned to read, write, and speak perfect Dutch, Edith gave up trying, even after a neighbour offered to help. Thereafter she spoke it badly and with a strong German accent. Both girls made fun of her, and Anne resented her mother speaking German, the language of Nazis.

A permanent bitterness was slowly settling over Edith.

She needed something to make her feel more secure and she turned to her religion. Margot joined her mother when she went to the synagogue and developed her own interest in Zionism. The Zionist philosophy of creating a homeland in Palestine for Jews from all over the world appealed to many young Jews. She also went to Hebrew school, something Anne, supported by her equally non-religious father, refused to do.

Margot and Edith became closer as Anne drifted further and further away from her mother.

Otto and Edith's unpretentious elegance and genuine hospitality made their apartment the place to be. Margot's and Anne's friends loved to visit.

Despite her personal torments, Edith made sure that her home was just that, a home — with all the warmth that implies. She prepared excellent meals — stews and wursts — and delicious treats: strawberry tarts, rolls topped with cream cheese and chocolate bits, and cornflakes with grated apples and cream. She served cold lemonade and bottled milk when everyone else had their milk put into a can by the grocers and brought back to the house. Everyone loved the lazy Susan that sat in the middle of the large circular dining room table so you could spin it around and take whatever food you wanted.

Otto always had time for the kids. He tried (unsuccessfully) to teach Lies to ride her bike and successfully to feed her little sister — a famously difficult task — chatting away amiably all the while.

The Franks' apartment became a social centre for the adults in the area also. Miep and her fiancé, Jan, the van Pelses (Hermann, his wife, Auguste "Gusti", and their son, Peter, who was Margot's age), Friedrich "Fritz" Pfeffer, a dentist, the Ledermanns, and the Goslars.

Edith and Ruth Goslar often went to the synagogue together, and the two families frequently celebrated the Friday night Sabbath meal at the Goslars'. Edith welcomed the Goslars' religious observance while Otto and Anne respectfully (only sometimes in Anne's case) endured it. Margot soaked up the talk about Zionism and moving to Palestine, something the Goslars hoped to do one day.

The van Pelses, Ledermanns, Goslars, and Fritz Pfeffer had much in common. Like the Franks they had all fled Germany and feared the future. Otto pointed out during these dinner discussions that Holland had remained neutral during the First World War. He was sure they would continue with that policy. But privately he worried that the Germans would attack despite Holland's declared neutrality.

Increasingly they talked about the anti-Jewish laws that were being passed in Germany and the worsening situation there.

On the morning of November 8, 1938, they read about a seventeen-year-old German-born Jewish boy named Herschel Grynszpan. He had become enraged when he received a postcard from his distraught sister telling him that their parents, along with twelve thousand other Jews, had been forcibly taken from their homes in Germany and were being herded into "relocation camps" along the German-Polish border. Herschel was close to his family, and he decided that he would take revenge by killing a member of the German embassy in Paris (where he had fled to).

He left a note for his uncle:

> *My dear relatives, I couldn't do otherwise. God must forgive me. My heart bleeds when I think of our tragedy and that of the 12,000 Jews. I have to protest in a way that the whole world hears my protest, and this I intend to do.*
>
> *I beg your forgiveness.*
>
> HERSCHEL

Boldly claiming he had important documents to deliver, he bluffed his way into the office of an attaché named Ernst vom Rath. Firing at point-blank range five times, he hit his victim twice. The wounds proved fatal, and on November 9, 1938, vom Rath died.

The act was followed immediately by anti-Jewish rioting throughout Germany. Thousands of Jewish-owned stores and businesses and hundreds of homes and synagogues were destroyed and set on fire. People fleeing the burning buildings were shot. Thirty thousand Jewish men were arrested and sent to "labour camps", and hundreds were humiliated and murdered in the streets. An untold number committed suicide.

At the time a portion of the German population thought that the riots were a spontaneous reaction to the news of the assassination. But that was just Nazi propaganda. In fact, Adolf Hitler, top Nazi officials and the police had instigated and orchestrated *Kristallnacht*, the "Night of the Broken Glass", as it came to be called because of the shattered glass that littered the streets the morning after.

Herschel surrendered without a struggle and said:

*"The Jewish race has a right to live, and I do not understand all the sufferings that the Germans are inflicting upon them. If you are a Jew you can obtain nothing, attempt nothing, and hope for nothing. You are hunted like an animal. Why this martyrdom?*

*It was not with hatred or vengeance that I acted, but because of love for my parents and for my people who were subjected unjustly to outrageous treatment. Nevertheless, this act was distasteful to me and I deeply regret it. However, I had no other means of demonstrating my feelings. It was the constantly gnawing idea of the suffering of my race which dominated me. For twenty-eight years my parents resided in Hanover. They had set up a modest business which was destroyed overnight. They were stripped of everything and expelled. It is not, after all, a crime to be Jewish. I am not a dog. I have the right to live. My people have a right to live on this earth."*

His trial was eventually called off, and although it is assumed Germans killed him there is no evidence. His fate remains unknown to this day.

In September 1939, the German army invaded Poland, revealing that the policy of appeasement that England and France had followed was a failure. They had allowed Germany to re-arm and mobilise militarily and invade foreign territories and countries (Austria and Czechoslovakia), all clear violations of the Treaty of Versailles. Hitler's continued military aggression, now into Poland, forced the two countries to declare war on Germany.

# *Occupation*

≡ 1940–1942 ≡

In the early morning hours of May 10, 1940, the German army attacked neutral Holland with no warning. They attacked Belgium, Luxembourg, and France that same day. Queen Wilhelmina came on the radio, which everyone was desperately listening to, and promised that Holland would not give up without a fight. She advised the population to remain calm. Three days later the queen was forced to flee to the relative safety of England. She continued to broadcast from London, assuring her country that the government would never compromise with Hitler and never give up.

There were conflicting reports in the early stages of the invasion. Telephone service was interrupted and people panicked, rushing to shops to stock up on food and running crazily in the streets trying to find out what was actually happening.

Some Jewish residents headed for the harbour, trying to board boats for England. Few got out.

German planes bombed Rotterdam, destroying the central part of the city, and dropped leaflets on Amsterdam warning that they would be next. On May 14, 1940, four days after the invasion began, the Dutch government surrendered and Holland was neutral no more.

German soldiers marched in the streets of Amsterdam.

The Franks, along with 130,000 other Jews in Holland, were trapped.

Within weeks local Dutch Nazi groups were insisting that Jewish-owned shops identify themselves. By the end of the year there were signs in coffeehouses, cafes, and restaurants saying that Jews were not welcome.

Beginning in 1941 and lasting for the next two years, a long list of anti-Jewish restrictions was put into effect.

≡ All Jews in Holland had to register with the authorities. Their identification books had a large J stamped on them.

≡ All businesses owned by Jews were to be reported. Jewish doctors and dentists were no longer allowed to treat Christians. Many placed ads in newspapers and magazines soliciting business from Jews to make up for the loss of their Christian patients.

≡ Restrictions were placed on the amount of money, jewellery, and precious objects Jews could own. Wedding rings, pocket watches, and four pieces of silverware per person were allowed.

≡ Parks, tennis courts, swimming pools, beaches, zoos, theatres, cinemas, museums, and libraries were off-limits.

≡ Owning radios, riding in cars, using public transport and owning a bicycle were forbidden. Even walking was restricted. There was no travelling without a permit, certain streets were designated as Jewish streets, and there was a 6.00 p.m. to 8.00 a.m. curfew.

≡ Shopping was confined to the hours of 3.00 p.m. to 5.00 p.m. and only in Jewish-owned shops.

≡ Jewish children were no longer allowed to attend school with Christian children — they would have to go to their own schools.

Faced with the overwhelming military power of the Germans, the majority of Jews and Christians cooperated. They feared that if they didn't things would get worse. And they hoped that if they did they could live through it.

Brave speeches by the Dutch government in exile and by England's combative and courageous Prime Minister Winston Churchill were intended to keep up morale. And there were reasons for hope. Hitler's plans for a quick conquest of Russia were stalled in the face of fierce resistance and the punishing Russian winter. After being attacked at Pearl Harbor on December 7, 1941, by Japan (Germany's ally), the United States had entered the war. Surely an invasion of Europe would come any day now. Surely the war would be over soon.

But day after day, week after week, Holland's Jewish population was being identified, isolated, and persecuted.


"Enjoy what there is" was one of Edith's favourite expressions. Now the Frank family struggled to do just that: to maintain a semblance of normal life in the increasingly anti-Jewish atmosphere of occupied Holland.

Margot continued with her Hebrew classes and joined a Zionist youth organisation. There she talked with her friends about the anti-Jewish laws that were being passed.

They also debated their faith in God and the pride or shame they felt because they were Jewish.

Otto Frank, tenaciously clinging to his belief that Germany was the home of Goethe and Schiller and not Hitler and Goebbels, hired a journalist to give Margot and her friends lessons in German literature.

Somehow Margot managed to concentrate on her schoolwork and continued to earn excellent grades. She tried not to show how worried she was but her stomach problem betrayed her inner turmoil.

In April 1940, Anne and Margot continued writing to their two American pen-pal sisters, ten-year-old Juanita and fourteen-year-old Betty Wagner. (Otto translated Anne's and Margot's letters into English.)

*Dear Juanita,*

*I did receive your letter and want to answer you as quick as possible. Margot and myself are the only children in our house. Our grandma is living with us. My father has an office and mother is busy at home. I live not far from school and I am sitting in the fifth class. We have no hour-classes we may do what we prefer, of course we* must get to a certain goal. Your mother will certainly know this system, it is called Montessori. We have little work at home.

On the map I looked and again found the name Burlington. I did ask a girl friend of mine if she would like to communicate with one of your friends. She wants to do it with a girl about my age not with a boy.

I shall write her address underneath. Did you yourself write the letter I received from you, or did your mother do it? I include a post-card from Amsterdam and shall continue to do that collecting picture-cards I have already about 800. A child I used to be at school with went to New-York and she did write a letter to our class some time ago. In case you and Betty get a photo do send a copy as I am curious to know how you look. My birthday is the 12th of June. Kindly let me know yours. Perhaps one of your friends wil [sic] write first to my girl friend, for she also cannot write English but her father or mother will translate the letter.

Hoping to hear from you I remain

*your Dutch friend*

ANNELIES MARIE FRANK

Anne enclosed a letter from Margot for Betty:

*Dear Betty Ann,*

*I have only received your letter about a week ago and had no time to answer right away. It is Sunday today, so I can take the time to write. During the week I am very busy as I have to work for school at home every day.*

*Our school begins at 9 a.m. till noon then I go home by my bicycle (if the weather is bad I go by bus and stay at school) and return for class beginning at half past one; we then have clas [sic] until three o'clock. Wednesday and Sunday afternoons we are free and use our time to play tennis and row. In the winter we play hockey or go skating if it is could [sic] enough. This year it was unusually cold and all the canals were frozen; today is the first really spring day, the sun shining bright and warm. Generally we have lots of rain.*

*In the summer we have a two months holiday, then a fortnight at Christmas and so on Easter; Whitsuntide only four days.*

*We often listen to the radio, as times are very exciting, having a frontier with Germany and being a small country we never feel safe. In our class most of the children communicate with one or the other so I do not know* children who would want to take up correspondence. I have two cousins, boy living at Basel, Switserland [sic]. For American ideas this is not far but for us it is. We have to travel through Germany which we cannot do or through Belgium and France and in that we cannot either. It is war and no visas are given.

We live in a five room flat attached to the only skyscraper of the city being twelve storeys high! Amsterdam has about 800,000 inhabitants. We are near the sea shore but we miss hills and woods. Everything being flat and a great part of the country lying below sea level, therefore the name Netherland.

Father is going to business in the morning and returns about 6 p.m.; Mother is busy at home. My grand-mother is living with us and we rented one room to a lady.

Now I think I have told you quite a lot and am expecting your answer.

With kindest regards
your friend
MARGOT BETTI FRANK

P.S. Many thanks for Juanita's letter as Anne is writing to her I need to write myself.

MARGOT

Anne had been sad to leave her Montessori school and the teachers were equally sad to see her go. But she enjoyed her new Jewish school. She and Lies were still together, but Sanne went to a different Jewish school. The two girls walked to school each morning and, although not initially in the same class, contrived to end up together.

Anne made another good friend in her new school, Jacqueline van Maarsen, who was called Jackie. They met the first day of school when Anne pedalled her bicycle next to Jackie and suggested that they ride home together. Within days they agreed on being best friends.

Jackie had also previously attended a Montessori school, (not Anne's), and Anne liked her for lots of reasons. She collected picture postcards of movie stars and also liked the Joop ter Heul series of books that was about a girl just like them. They read sections aloud and acted out scenes for each other. In addition, Jackie was quite knowledgeable about boys and other things, thanks to her informative older sister. Anne tried to talk to Margot (whose fully developed figure she was jealous of) and her mother about sex, but both were reluctant to discuss it with her. Her father pretended to discuss it but basically dodged the issue.

Jackie didn't leave with Anne for school in the morning because Jackie was invariably late. However, she accompanied

Anne when Anne went to be tutored in maths and waited outside for her until she had finished.

Reserved Jackie appreciated Anne's assertiveness, honesty, and sense of humour. Once when Anne came for a sleepover she brought, along with her cosmetic case filled with hair curlers, an empty suitcase. She just didn't feel like she was truly travelling unless she had a suitcase with her. Another time, when they were having dinner, Anne abruptly announced that she had to go and bathe her cat, Moortje. When someone pointed out that cats really didn't like to be bathed, Anne, clearly considering the remark preposterous, said that she had bathed her a number of times and Moortje never once uttered a word of protest.

And they talked about the Germans, about what had happened to their lives, and about how scared they were. Jackie told Anne about how embarrassed she was when she wasn't allowed in the pool along with the rest of her swimming club. And about her cousin David who had, they recently learned, died in one of those so-called labour camps.

Unlike Jackie, who enjoyed being alone, Anne needed to have someone around. And even though she had three very good friends and an ever wider circle of acquaintances, she worried that she didn't have that one true best friend, that one special person she could talk to about her innermost feelings.

Anne read a lot — Greek and Roman mythology and genealogy were her favourite areas of study. In school she did well in subjects she liked, but in others like maths (which she had to repeat in year six), she struggled to get good grades and to pay attention in class.

Her maths teacher, despite his good sense of humour, was annoyed with Anne's social activities during class. He made her write two essays, hoping to break her of the habit of talking while he was lecturing. One was entitled "A Chatterbox." Anne's essay contended that talking was a feminine characteristic and something she had inherited from her mother, and therefore she could do little about.

Her maths teacher appreciated Anne's irresistible sense of humour and genuine writing talent but not that she continued to talk just as she had done before. The third time he assigned a five-hundred-word essay entitled "Quack, Quack, Quack, Said Mistress Chatterbox."

With characteristic flair, Anne turned the punishment into an opportunity to be creative and, equally important, to be in the limelight. She wrote a charming poem (with help from her poetic friend Sanne) about a mother and father duck and their baby ducks — who chattered too much. Her maths teacher read the poem out loud, adding his own comments, not only to Anne's class but to others.

Of course he was not aware that behind his back Anne referred to teachers in general as "the biggest freaks on earth".

After school, Anne and her friends did their homework in the Franks' sitting room; Lies couldn't work at home because of her insistent little sister. They also played Monopoly in the living room and made sandwiches in the kitchen while feeding Moortje.

Anne enjoyed being popular and the centre of attention, something her upbeat personality entitled her to. She drew people to her like a magnet; they wanted to be with her and around her. She and her friends formed a table tennis club, since one of them had a table at home and table tennis was one of the few activities not yet banned by the Nazis. After meetings they went to the Cafe Delphi or the Oasis, an ice-cream parlour whose owners were Jewish. They had strawberry ice cream that they ate outside on the pavement while they watched the boys go by.

Boys interested Anne much more than homework. With her piercing, probing, grey-green cat eyes and intensely-serious-one-minute, hopelessly-playful-the-next openly flirtatious personality, Anne was popular with boys, especially older boys.

She was younger than her first two boyfriends, Peter Schiff and Hello Silverberg. Hello's grandfather disliked the boy's given name, Helmuth, and had mercifully bestowed Hello upon him. Hello and Anne were introduced by his cousin. Hello had a girlfriend at the time but once he met Anne, the other faded. Hello's friends and his grandmother (whom he lived with) considered Anne much too young for worldly sixteen-year-old Hello. Hello thought Anne's friends were childish, and Anne told him she agreed. He was attracted by her unique personality and insatiably curious mind — an attraction that was only emphasised by her alleged youth. He accompanied her to school at times and they went on walks together, talking about everything under the sun.

Otto and Edith liked Hello: he was good-looking and well-behaved. Margot agreed; the two of them having in common the Zionist meetings they attended. And Hello fully appreciated the Franks' gracious hospitality and genuine interest in him.


Anne wanted her thirteenth birthday to be extra special. Something to take her mind off the ever-encroaching darkness of the outside world.

Being deprived of going to the cinema was a particular hardship for Anne, who loved films and closely followed the careers and private lives of her favourite film stars. She could easily rattle off who was in what film and what year, throwing in the reviews as well. She even fantasised about some day being a film star herself.

The Franks regularly rented movies and a projector and had the girls and their friends over, Otto on projector and Edith on refreshments.

That was the plan for Anne's birthday party. Anne and Jackie created official-looking invitations with the precise time, row and seat number, and warning that this was strictly invitation only.

Then they gave them out to everyone: friends, neighbours, classmates, and Margot's friends. This year, for the first time, everyone was Jewish. Some of Anne's former friends in the neighbourhood were now wearing the uniform of the Dutch Nazi Youth Movement.

After dinner and a delicious dessert (one of Edith's strawberry tarts) the shades were pulled down and a film about a dog who rescues a lighthouse keeper was shown.

Anne received lots of gifts — as if to compensate for the grim reality outside — a blue blouse, Variety (the latest Monopoly-like board game), books, two brooches, and carnations from Hello.

But for Anne the highlight of her birthday was the diary she had wanted. Anne had decided with certainty that she wanted to be a writer, preferably a famous one. She had seen the diary in Blankevoorts, her favourite bookshop. It was really one of the autograph books she, Lies, and Sanne had been writing poetry in for years. The one she wanted was square with a checked cloth cover and an oval clasp with a strap so she could lock it. She was going to write in it with her favourite fountain pen, the one her grandmother had given her.

Pim got the diary for her, as she knew he would. That was all that really mattered.

Otto made the adjustments necessary to continue his business. Because of another new regulation, he changed the name and legal ownership so that it was free of Jews, on paper at least. In reality he continued to run it as he always had.

The company had moved into its new headquarters at 263 Prinsengracht, right along the canal. It was a four-storey building with double doors opening from the street into the warehouse. There were offices on the second floor and storage on the third and fourth. After a while they had expanded to the annexe behind the front building. The two buildings were connected by a corridor.

Always plagued by an inner nervousness, Otto struggled mightily not to show the strain of walking the two miles back and forth to the office every day, of worrying about the business, of worrying about the fate of his family.

He and Edith tried to protect their children from what was happening in the world around them but it was impossible. They knew that Mr Ledermann had already burned all the books he owned that were written by Jewish and other now-forbidden authors, fearing that possessing them might bring even more trouble. And there was nothing they could do to prevent the girls from hearing German military vehicles rumbling in the streets below their windows or the unnerving sound of night bombers as the British planes flew over Holland on their way to attacking German cities.

Otto assured Margot and Anne that Mr Goslar's views were wrong — Germany would not win the war. America would not allow that to happen, Otto explained. And they believed him.

And they believed Edith was right as well when she told them to "enjoy what there is". They tried to look at things as positively as they could. Walking was good for your health. They didn't have to go to cinemas to see films; they could watch at home. If they couldn't go to concert halls to hear music, they could go to Sanne's house and hear her parents play. Not being able to swim or play tennis in the summer or skate in the winter wasn't the worst thing in the world, was it?

In late April 1942, all Jews were required to wear a six-pointed Star of David made of yellow fabric with *Jood* (Jew) in black letters mocking Hebrew writing. The star could be obtained at distribution stations throughout Amsterdam and had to be paid for with ration stamps.

The star had to be sewn on — merely fastening it with a pin was a punishable offence — and placed breast high on the left side of an outer garment. It was to be worn at all times when outside (even on the balcony or backyard of your home).

One part of Amsterdam became known as Hollywood, another the Milky Way, because of so many stars seen there.

Many Dutch Christians also wore the star and yellow flowers to show their support. They considered this a shameful chapter in their country's long liberal history. After they were beaten by the increasingly brutal German soldiers and Dutch Nazis, their show of solidarity evaporated.

Some were not so sympathetic. They were glad to see the hated Jews finally getting what was coming to them.

Teachers in the Jewish schools did their best to convince their beleaguered students that they should look upon the stars as a badge of honour and not a sign of shame.

Little children seeing their older brothers and sisters wearing the star complained that they also wanted to wear one.

The star visibly marked the Jews of Holland.

As always, there were lies, rumours, misinformation and self-delusion. They were just being taken to a labour camp. The Germans needed their labour because the war was taking so many of their men. Since they were needed to perform this important labour, surely they would be treated properly. Life in the labour camps wasn't so bad, some said. The work was hard, but there was at least enough food. The circular the Germans issued minimalised the threat. They said bring books, writing materials, postcards to write home, so how bad could it be?

But why had no one returned from these so-called labour camps, others asked. And what of the rumours that they were murdered there?

When the roundups first began there were warnings. People were able to sneak out to a friend's for a few nights if they knew they were on the list. Now that they had so obediently registered — just a formality, they were told — the notices for the call-ups were being sent via registered post to their homes. Now the Jewish stars they were required to wear made them that much easier to identify. Now there was nowhere to hide.

Some looked to the Amsterdam Jewish Council for guidance. The Council claimed to be working with the Germans, helping them to communicate with the Jewish community. They were, they said, attempting to make the best of things. They urged compliance, not resistance, as the only wise path to take.

But some said the Jewish Council was looking out for themselves and their well-connected friends and they cared nothing for the rest of the Jewish population. They were collaborating with the Germans and saving their own skins, that's all.

No one was quite sure what the truth was and no one quite knew what to do.

One thing was certain: the roundups were tearing families apart, literally.

The teenagers who were being called up were old enough and smart enough to think for themselves. Some wanted to go, telling their distraught parents that they were strong, that working in a labour camp was something they could handle. By going they hoped to spare their parents further hardship.

But sometimes it was just the opposite. The child did not want to go but the parents insisted, afraid that if the child didn't go, the entire family would be jeopardised.

Some families chose another alternative. Whole families took an overdose of sleeping pills, sliced their wrists open, or closed the windows and turned on the gas.

The Franks had hoped they had put all this behind them nine years ago when they left Frankfurt. Now they knew that it had followed them.

Like thousands of other families they agonised over their limited choices.

Edith wanted to leave. But if they left Holland where would they go? Was Switzerland safer than Holland? Should they go to Palestine? Who knew what was there? Peru? Argentina? What about America?

They knew that the forbidding and complex American immigration laws were nearly impossible to overcome. The quota system wouldn't let them in unless they had an American sponsor — someone who would guarantee that they wouldn't arrive destitute and have to be supported by the government. And even if by some small miracle they did get visas, how would they live once they got there? How would Otto make a living? How would his family survive?

Some parents were sending their children out of the country without them, even sending siblings to separate places, as a further precaution in a world gone insane.

Otto and Edith discussed sending the girls to live with relatives in England but couldn't do it. The family must not be separated, this much they agreed on.

They would remain in Holland. That was the best choice. That was their best chance. Otto was certain, even if Edith was not. Like so many other Jews trapped in occupied Holland, they would go into hiding. But time was running out. If they didn't go soon it might be too late.

Otto knew just where they could go. He had been thinking about it and working on it for months. It was an audacious and, therefore, risky plan. But it was the only one that would allow him to continue to earn money and keep the family together. Soon everything would be ready. By July 16 they could go into hiding.

Sunday, July 5, 1942, was a sunny summer day. Anne was on the back terrace reading and soaking up the sun while her sister and mother were inside. Otto had gone out and was expected back around five.

At three o'clock the postman arrived with a registered letter. It was from the Central Office for Jewish Immigration and was notification that Margot was to report so she could be taken to a labour camp. The order said she should bring a blanket, food, towels, sheets, toilet articles, a plate, cup, spoon, winter shoes, socks, two pairs of underpants, overalls, and a suitcase or backpack with her name, birth date, and "Holland" marked on it.

When Otto returned and Edith showed him the notice he knew immediately that they couldn't wait until July 16. He had told Margot and Anne that they might have to go into hiding, it was just sooner than expected. His calm explanation did little to reduce his daughters' fears.

Otto wanted to go into hiding with Hermann van Pels and his family. But Edith wanted to be with the Goslars. Otto pointed out that Gabi was too small, and to make matters even more complicated, Ruth Goslar was pregnant. They couldn't consider going into hiding with a small child and an infant.

But that wasn't the only reason Otto chose the van Pels family. One of Otto's main concerns was seeing to it that the business kept running, kept making much-needed money for him and his family. Hermann van Pels was essential to that plan, and he would no doubt want his family to join Otto's in hiding. There was really no choice.

Now time was up. They would have to go — even if the preparations were not quite complete. Everyone who worked for Otto in the office — Kleiman, Kugler, Bep, and Miep — knew what to do. The trust and good will that had developed between Otto Frank and his employees over the past nearly ten years was about to be put to the ultimate test. He would be relying on them to save his life and the lives of his family.

And they too would be risking a great deal. Anyone caught helping Jews in hiding would be sent to prison, or worse. Otto had already spoken to each of them, and each had agreed without hesitation to do whatever was required.

For weeks they had helped carry in supplies, a little at a time: canned goods, dried vegetables, clothes, bedding, sheets, towels, cooking utensils, eating implements, dishes, and rugs. Furniture from the residences of the Franks and van Pelses had been "sent out to be upholstered" (so the children wouldn't suspect anything) but was really moved on weekends, at night.

Miep had been preparing for the difficult task of buying the food each day. A task made even harder by rationing and by buying for so many people — and not just people — Jews in hiding. She would have to be sure not to shop at the same stores so that no one became suspicious. Hermann van Pels had taken her with him numerous times to a butcher he knew well. He wanted the butcher to recognise Miep so he would give her extra rations for them when they were in hiding. Although Miep wondered why he would go to a butcher near the office rather than where he lived, she said nothing.

Jan and Miep (who were married by now) came over at eleven o'clock that Sunday evening. They put on layers of

Otto's and Edith's clothing and stuffed as much as they dared under their raincoats and into their pockets. After they unburdened themselves they came back for another load.

Anne wanted to know where they were going to hide, but her father would not tell her, even now.

Mr Goldschmidt, who rented the large apartment upstairs from the Franks, decided this was a good time for a visit. His presence forced them to act as if nothing out of the ordinary was happening, an added strain on an already eerie evening.

As frightened as Anne was, she was so emotionally drained that she went right to sleep. At 5.30 a.m. Monday morning, her mother woke her up.

At 6.00, as agreed, Miep returned to take Margot. Her satchel was filled with schoolbooks and she was wearing four layers of clothing, but not her yellow star.

Miep had brought her bike over the night before. Margot had not turned hers in (as Jews had been required to do) because her parents thought it might be useful in an emergency.

Margot usually rode fast but that morning she pedalled at an even, unhurried pace, hoping to give the impression that Miep and she were just two Dutch working girls on their way to their jobs, as usual, on a Monday.

Margot had no idea where Miep was taking her.

Meanwhile Otto, Edith and Anne readied themselves to leave. Otto left a purposely misleading note for Mr Goldschmidt, one that would lead him to think they had departed for Switzerland. And it asked that a neighbour take care of Moortje, the cat.

They left the breakfast dishes uncleared, the beds unmade, and clothes scattered all over. All to further give the impression of a sudden, hurried leave-taking.

They too wore layers of clothing as well as hats and scarves. Anne carried her stuffed schoolbag, having packed her precious diary first, then hair curlers, a comb, schoolbooks and some letters. As they walked through the steaming summer rain, Otto told Anne where they were going.

It was 7.30 a.m.

Cars drove by without stopping, knowing it was too dangerous to offer Jews a lift.

By then Miep had already brought Margot to the hiding place: 263 Prinsengracht. They would be hiding in the empty annexe of their father's office building. The rear-building annexe was connected to the front one by a narrow corridor and a staircase. It could not be seen from the street. They would be living on the second and third floors and in the attic space.

Although terrified and nearly in shock from enduring the past twenty-four hours, Margot showed no emotion. Soaked by the rain, Miep and she put their bicycles in the storeroom.

Miep led Margot up the stairs, past her father's office, up the stairway to the landing that led to the hiding place. Leaving Margot there, Miep returned to her desk.

Upstairs, alone, in the annexe hiding place, sixteen-year-old Margot waited for her parents and her thirteen-year-old sister to join her.

# PART TWO

# HIDING

# The Diary of Margot Frank

## ≡ A RE-CREATION ≡
### JULY 6, 1942–JULY 31, 1944

MONDAY, JULY 6, 1942

I wish I could stop crying but I can't. It was all I could do to control myself on the way over here.

I'm so frightened.

The seconds pass by like hours and the walls feel as if they are closing in on me. I hope Daddy, Mummy, and Anne come soon.

WEDNESDAY, JULY 8, 1942

Daddy and Anne have been working for the past two days. Laying out the rolled-up rugs; moving furniture around; unpacking boxes; putting away pots, pans and dishes; taking the clothes that are piled high on the beds and sorting them; sewing together material to make crude curtains for the windows and tacking them up. They've even scrubbed the kitchen floor.

Two busy little bees, chatting away as if there is nothing out of the ordinary going on here. As if we're on holiday and about to have the time of our lives.

It is all I can do just to lie here quietly, trying to gather my strength. Like Mummy I have been unable to eat anything.

THURSDAY, JULY 9, 1942

Since the occupation there hasn't been a day when I didn't feel the overwhelming burden of having to cope. Actually, it is quite remarkable how many compromises you can make; how much you can adjust to and still say you are enjoying your life.

This is even worse than when we had to leave Frankfurt. I don't remember being this frightened then. Perhaps I was too young to fully realise all that was happening. Now, unlike then, we are not going to something — to another country where we hoped to live in peace. Now we are running from something. We are "undergrounders", as the Dutch say. Like common criminals we are in hiding. As if we did something we ought to be ashamed of. As if being Jewish were a crime.

I do my best not to break under the strain. Daddy has enough on his mind. But just thinking about it makes me shudder.

I keep hoping this is some grotesque nightmare from which I will soon awake. I feel crushed by the weight of it all. We will never overcome the hardships that have been so unjustly heaped on us. Why do people hate us because we are Jewish? Even Daddy cannot adequately explain it to me, and as much as I read, I still can't fathom where all the hatred comes from.

FRIDAY, JULY 10, 1942

Anne was ecstatic that Daddy thought to bring her picture postcard collection of film stars. She has the energy of a thousand people and has wasted no time pasting them up. Her collection is so vast they now cover one entire wall of our small room. It does make it decidedly less dreary.

Daddy and Mummy are right next door. Mummy is trying her best but she takes everything too much to heart. She burned the pea soup rather badly, which I think is making her feel even worse.

SATURDAY, JULY 11, 1942

Not only did I break the vacuum cleaner but something "blew" when I pulled out the plug cord from the socket, and now we have no light.

I have a bad cold. Cycling here in the rain didn't help matters, I'm sure. In addition, the building is quite damp. No matter how much codeine Mummy gives me it doesn't go away. I am forbidden to cough for fear of someone hearing.

SUNDAY, JULY 12, 1942

Tomorrow the van Pels family will arrive. We will have to accommodate living in these confined quarters with a whole other family. I can't even imagine what it's going to be like.

Daddy likes Mr van Pels and enjoys his jokes. Mrs van Pels is humorous in her own way. I don't know where their son, Peter, gets his shyness from, certainly not his parents.

TUESDAY, JULY 14, 1942

The van Pels family arrived yesterday.

Mrs van Pels shamelessly carted along her chamber pot that she had concealed in a hatbox. She displayed it proudly for all to see before placing it safely under her bed. Mr van Pels brought his folding tea table and Peter his cat — which I don't quite understand because we were not allowed to bring ours.

Mr van Pels told us what happened after we left our apartment last week. Mr Goldschmidt read the note Daddy "accidentally" left and reacted just as he hoped: Mr Goldschmidt thinks we have gone off to Switzerland. Some of the neighbours said they saw all of us cycling away in the early morning hours and another said we had been taken away by a military van in the middle of the night.

Mr van Pels told Anne about Lies and Jackie coming to call and how shocked and saddened they were to find that she and her family had vanished. They wanted to have something to remember her by so they took her swimming medals, even though they knew the Germans forbid anyone from removing anything from a house in which Jews have lived. It appears anything we leave behind they want for themselves.


SUNDAY, JULY 19, 1942

Miep and her new husband came to celebrate their first anniversary with us. Mrs van Pels prepared a delicious meal and created a rather humorous menu as a keepsake. Anne named the restaurant "The Annexe" and invented witty names for each course. One was named after the street the

59

Gieses live on and another after their butcher. They stayed the night, which was quite an exciting event for us.

## THURSDAY, JULY 23, 1942

As I said it is astonishing the things you can adjust to and still maintain your equilibrium.

I wake at seven o'clock, the latest, and wait patiently in line to use our one bathroom. Everyone *must* finish their morning ritual before eight-thirty, when the warehouse workers arrive and the office is open for business.

After eight-thirty we have to keep our voices low, almost a whisper, and walk around in slippers or stockinged feet. This is so that none of the warehouse workers downstairs or businesspeople who happen to come by the office will know we are here. No running water and no using the bathroom (we have to use jam jars in the meantime).

During the midday break, when the warehouse workers are out having lunch, we can move around a little more freely, turn on the tap, and use the toilet. That's when Miep, Bep, Mr Kugler and Mr Kleiman come for visit. Mr Kugler and Mr Kleiman bring Daddy much-needed information about the business so he can continue to make important decisions. Mr Kleiman brings bread (he knows someone who owns lots of bakeries) and books, a rather appropriate combination. Every Monday Mr Kugler brings Anne her precious *Cinema and Theater* magazine. Bep brings the milk and Miep gets the shopping list for the day, while Anne pesters her for news, any news, about friends, neighbours, anything, and everything.

At five-thirty, when the workday is over, someone comes up and gives us the all clear. Then we can walk around, flush the toilet, luxuries like that. We eat every meal upstairs in what is the van Pelses' bedroom by night, but our communal kitchen-living room by day.

Most evenings we go downstairs and listen to the BBC news from London on the radio in Daddy's office. At nine we move all the chairs out of the way, pull out the beds (Anne's is so short that she has to use a chair to extend it), and distribute the sheets and blankets, thereby converting our living quarters into sleeping quarters.

TUESDAY, JULY 28, 1942

It is nearly impossible to find somewhere quiet during the day. Somewhere I don't have to listen to anyone's complaining or arguing. I read and do my schoolwork and shut out the rest as best I can.

FRIDAY, AUGUST 7, 1942

Mummy and I light the Sabbath candles.


TUESDAY, AUGUST 18, 1942

I wish Mr van Pels would stop badgering me about my appetite, or lack of. Frankly I can't imagine why anyone would have one, considering.

The other night we had meat and eels and Mr van Pels asked me why I didn't put some meat on my bread. Then Anne took some cheese and Mr van Pels said that she couldn't have it because cheese was only for those who ate their meat, or some such thing. Then, of course, Anne and Mr van Pels were off and running at the mouth. Anne loves to argue with adults.


SUNDAY, AUGUST 23, 1942

Mummy and Anne got into an argument about, of all things, barley soup. Anne complained that it was too hot, and Mummy said that Anne never eats anything that is too hot. Then Mummy insisted that Anne eat the meat that was in the soup, and Anne refused. Then Mr van Pels said something — I don't even remember what it was (I try not to listen to half of what goes on at dinner). I was trying to cut the fat off my meat and Anne got cross because no one was saying anything about that, my cutting the fat away, and she went on about how everyone always picks on her.

I wanted to scream.

TUESDAY, AUGUST 25, 1942

Bep's father built a bookcase in front of the door that reveals the stairway that leads up to where we're hiding. It has concealed hinges so it can be swung open and will be filled with old-looking file folders from the office to further obscure the entrance.

WEDNESDAY, AUGUST 26, 1942

Anne has worked herself into a state because Peter and I are allowed to read books that she isn't, due to her age. She thinks Daddy and Mummy treat her like a baby and don't realise that she's not a child any more. I must say she has a point. On the other hand, Anne doesn't like to be told no to anything, no matter what it is.

THURSDAY, AUGUST 27, 1942

More Frank-van Pels arguments over inconsequential issues such as who's using whose bed linen and dinner plates. Anne broke one of Mrs van Pels's soup bowls, which

63

led to accusations (somewhat valid) that Anne is not careful or considerate.

Daddy does his best to remain above the fray, quietly reading his beloved Dickens.

FRIDAY, SEPTEMBER 4, 1942

Anne is knitting a sweater and working on Daddy's family tree. I spent most of the afternoon peeling potatoes and scrubbing pots and pans with Mummy.

There is no more butter.

MONDAY, SEPTEMBER 14, 1942

Bep told us that one of Anne's friends was deported with her family. Usually our visitors try not to tell us too much bad news from the outside world. And the newspapers they bring are heavily censored by the Germans. Still, we are able to piece it together and we can guess how bad it is.

WEDNESDAY, SEPTEMBER 16, 1942

Mrs van Pels is constantly on at Anne about her endless chattering. Although she has a point, that's simply the way Anne is and nothing on earth is going to make her change.

THURSDAY, SEPTEMBER 17, 1942

Mr Pfeffer may be coming into hiding with us. I have met him once or twice when he came to the house and he seems quite pleasant, if somewhat standoffish. Miep says he's very intelligent and a good dentist.

SUNDAY, SEPTEMBER 20, 1942

Anne is working on her French irregular verbs while I tend to my studies. I want to make sure I keep up because I don't want to have any difficulties when I return to school.

MONDAY, SEPTEMBER 21, 1942

I am being driven to distraction by that awful Westerkerk clock that Anne is so fond of. The church is just down the street and it sounds off every fifteen minutes, mercilessly reminding me that I am trapped here and not at home, where I long to be.

TUESDAY, SEPTEMBER 22, 1942

Anne and I are helping Daddy to improve his Dutch, which is quite a chore. Peter is having difficulties with his English lessons.

SUNDAY, SEPTEMBER 27, 1942

More arguing, this time over the proper way to address employees. During the course of the discussion Anne told Mummy that she shouldn't say "servants", rather, she should say "household help". If that wasn't bad enough Anne had to add that "after the war" Mummy will have to adjust to changes like that.

Anne says "after the war" with annoying frequency and Mummy is, to put it mildly, not as optimistic as Anne is and so it has become a constant irritant. Mummy questions whether or not there is going to be an "after the war" soon or whether we will approve of its composition.

I find it all deeply disturbing.


TUESDAY, SEPTEMBER 29, 1942

Although it was quite difficult under the circumstances everyone tried to make Mrs van Pels's birthday a special occasion. We prepared a nice meal: tongue, cauliflower, potatoes, and apple tarts for dessert.

Anne put a fur on Daddy's head, which was funny, but then Mr. van Pels snatched my glasses from off my nose and he put the fur on, which was even funnier.

All the people in the office gave her something, as did our family. Her husband presented her with red carnations.

I dearly hope I don't have to celebrate my birthday here.

WEDNESDAY, SEPTEMBER 30, 1942

More bickering about petty things such as tea towels and vegetables — who is and isn't cleaning them, and who is and isn't eating theirs.

Mrs van Pels, it appears, has decided that Anne's eating habits are her concern. When Anne responds unkindly to her endless needling, Mrs van Pels accuses her of being spoiled. Daddy and Mummy usually don't respond, rightly considering that kind of thing beneath them. Daddy did, however, point out to Mrs van Pels that Anne has learned to tolerate her long speeches without interrupting, which he considers a sign of maturity. Daddy was using humour to make a point.

As if this whole discussion wasn't lowly enough, it sank even further with unsolicited descriptions of the various intestinal problems caused by eating vegetables, the details of which I would rather not record here.

SATURDAY, OCTOBER 3, 1942

Mummy and Anne are fighting again and this time Mummy started to cry. It doesn't help matters at all that Anne is so outspoken about preferring Daddy to Mummy. Anne must learn that, although she may feel strongly about something, some things are best left unspoken. Actually, it's my considered opinion that most things are best left unspoken.


SUNDAY, OCTOBER 4, 1942

Anne and I had a nice bath. We have to use the soap sparingly, of course, and there isn't actually a *bathtub*, just a washtub that's barely big enough. I enjoyed the soothing hot water and even more the feeling of finally being clean.

Each of us here prefers to take our baths in different places. Daddy in his office; Mummy and Peter in the kitchen; and Mr van Pels in his room. As far as I can tell, Mrs van Pels has chosen not to bathe thus far. One has to wonder what the future holds as far as that's concerned.

Anne and I take our bath downstairs in the front office. We don't like to bother hauling the water up the stairs (we have only cold water on our two floors), and besides, we like to be in the office on the weekends, when no one is there.

While one of us bathes, the other can (carefully) peek out from behind the curtains at the people visiting friends and going places. Anne enjoys looking out more than I do. I find it frustrating because it makes me think about my own friends, Barbara and Jettke, and what they're doing now.

MONDAY, OCTOBER 5, 1942

Bep brought Anne and I new skirts from Bijenkorf's, which was so thoughtful of her. The material is a bit on the rough side, which is typical of the wartime goods we have learned to accept.

Bep also set up a correspondence course in shorthand for the three of us that I am looking forward to.

TUESDAY, OCTOBER 6, 1942

Yesterday Anne and I were reading together and she talked about how anxious she is to start her period. I think my sister is too eager to rush through her youth, even though it's only just begun.

### Thursday, October 8, 1942

More unfortunate news from the world outside. They are searching houses without warning and picking up people in the middle of the night — a job made easier for the Nazis because of the yellow stars all the Jews must wear. Jews don't dare go out without them. One man was taken away recently just because he took the J off his identity card. Thousands have been seized and taken away in the recent roundups.

### Saturday, October 10, 1942

Miep and Mr Gies came to dinner and to spend the night. (Anne and I slept in Daddy and Mummy's room so the Gieses could have ours.) They are so brave. Miep pretends it's just the most normal thing in the world but we all know that the two of them, along with Mr Kugler, Mr Kleiman, and Bep, are risking their lives for us every day.

After the delicious dinner we prepared (topped off by spiced gingerbread, biscuits, and coffee), the men went down to listen to the radio. I don't like listening to the radio any more. The Germans have conquered half the world: Holland, Belgium, Norway, Denmark, Greece, France — will England soon succumb? There are barely believable reports about the Germans killing Jewish people in large numbers using machine guns and poison gas.

Here, in Holland, Nazis are taking hostages and every time a German soldier or official is shot or there is an act of sabotage, a number of the hostages are executed in retaliation. No one knows for certain even if there really have been acts of sabotage or if it's just an excuse to murder them in cold blood.

Miep told us about Westerbork, which is the labour camp eighty miles north of Amsterdam where they are taking all the Jews they round up. She said they don't have adequate food, water, or bathroom facilities there.

I can't remember the last time I slept through the night.


TUESDAY, OCTOBER 13, 1942

Peter and Anne dressed up the other night. Anne wore Peter's suit and Peter one of his mother's dresses. It gave everyone a much needed laugh. Peter is, I think, a bit odd.


WEDNESDAY, OCTOBER 14, 1942

Mummy and Anne are getting along a little better, which is a relief. Truthfully I don't think we can afford these petty squabbles. Our life is oppressive enough without them.

I for one refuse to participate.

### THURSDAY, OCTOBER 15, 1942

I was working on my shorthand when Daddy and Anne asked me to help them with one of Anne's maths problems. It had them both stumped. Honestly I didn't think it was that difficult and was surprised at Daddy.

### SATURDAY, OCTOBER 17, 1942

We weighed ourselves this morning and Anne is thrilled that she has gained so much weight — seventeen pounds. She does look healthy, considering. She asked if I wanted to help her with the office work she's doing and I declined, which I think annoyed her.

### SUNDAY, OCTOBER 18, 1942

Anne's finger hurts terribly so she is unable to do any ironing.

She was able, however, to put up some more photographs from her film star collection. She put them up with corners, so that they can be safely taken down "after the war". I do not know how she summons up the courage to think so positively all the time.

MONDAY, OCTOBER 19, 1942

Mr van Pels has decided he doesn't want to sit next to me at dinner any more because my eating habits, which are too discriminating for his tastes, are spoiling his appetite. I haven't seen any diminishment in his appetite. I'm surprised he can eat at all, given the fact that he never takes his cigarette out of his mouth. I think the severe cigarette rationing is the real source of his current irritable mood.

It's quite all right with me, the new seating arrangement, because now I sit next to Mummy, which I much prefer.

TUESDAY, OCTOBER 20, 1942

We had quite a scare this morning. No one told us that someone would be coming to fill the fire extinguishers in the building. Thus, without warning, we heard quite a commotion right outside the door that leads to the stairway — the one hidden by the bookcase. Bep, who was visiting with us at the time, was therefore trapped.

We couldn't very well let her go down the stairs while he was there. We all listened quietly, waiting for him to stop. At one point it sounded as if he was knocking on the bookcase, which petrified all of us. Finally we heard Mr Kleiman calling from the other side and knew it was safe.

As it turns out the hooks that allow the bookcase to be swung open had jammed, and no one could come up and warn us he was coming.

Our lives consist of hours of dread punctuated by bursts of pure panic.

WEDNESDAY, OCTOBER 21, 1942

Mrs van Pels and Anne have discovered something new to argue about: Mrs van Pels's rather obvious flirtation with Daddy. (Subtlety is not her strong suit.) She strokes his hair and reveals more of her leg than is appropriate or aesthetically pleasing.

Daddy, of course, pays no attention to Mrs van Pels, a minor factor that doesn't slow her down one bit.

THURSDAY, OCTOBER 22, 1942

For the past few nights Anne and I have lain in bed together and talked about all sorts of things. I'm not nearly as comfortable talking about some of these topics as Anne is, but my sister is not familiar with the concept of embarrassment. Brazen is her middle name.

Usually Anne just babbles on about her most favourite topic, herself, which is fine with me. She's almost always entertaining and diverting, if not profound. I don't particularly like talking about myself anyway. But this time Anne seemed genuinely interested in hearing what I thought.

She wanted to know what my plans for the future were. I think she talks about the future — "after the war" — so much because it keeps her from getting depressed.

I think she misinterpreted my hesitancy in responding as secretiveness. Anne thinks everyone is like her and knows precisely what they are going to do for the entire rest of their lives. Of course the fact that she frequently changes her mind — one day she wants to be a famous writer, the next a famous Hollywood movie queen (famous being the constant) — doesn't truly register.

I must admit I did enjoy talking to her about my plans to become a midwife and my dreams of someday settling in Palestine.

I asked her if I could read her diary, and much to my surprise, she agreed. Anne is very guarded about her diary. Even before we went into hiding she was like that. At school or at home, she would hide what she was writing from presumably prying eyes with her hands. Here, if anyone comes near while she is writing, she slams it shut. She is much more conscientious about her diary than I am about mine. She works on it in our room and Daddy and Mummy's — never upstairs.

She wanted to know if I thought she was pretty. I told her she was and that she has particularly nice eyes, but that didn't seem to satisfy her.

### FRIDAY, OCTOBER 23, 1942

Daddy began reading A Tale of Two Cities aloud. Now, too, it seems like the best of times and the worst of times. The best because of my family and friends and the life we had built in Amsterdam. The worst because of the Nazis who have ruined it all.

### THURSDAY, OCTOBER 29, 1942

Anne and I both had colds last week, and now Daddy is sick. He has a rash and a high fever. Mummy is hoping that the fever will sweat it out of him. Of course, we don't dare call a doctor.

## TUESDAY, NOVEMBER 3, 1942

"Only his daughter had the power of charming this black brooding from his mind. She was the golden thread that united him to a Past beyond his misery, and to a Present beyond his misery: and the sound of her voice, the light of her face, the touch of her hand, had a strong, beneficial influence with him almost always. Not absolutely always, for she could recall some occasions on which her power had failed; but they were few and slight, and she believed them over."

— DICKENS

## MONDAY, NOVEMBER 9, 1942

I was immersed in a book — reading is the only thing that takes my mind off my dismal surroundings. I put it down and went upstairs to get something to eat. When I returned Anne had picked up my book and was looking at the drawings in it.

Anne is easily bored due in large part to her microscopically short attention span — especially if she hasn't taken her valerian. She is always ferreting around for something to relieve her boredom, so she stumbled upon my book. The fact that I was reading it was of no concern to her.

Anne, who, with good reason, seems even moodier and more sensitive since we came here, apparently felt that the tone of voice I used to ask for it back was offensive or inappropriate in some way. She ignored me and continued to peruse the drawings at her leisure.

Mummy admonished Anne for her childish behavior and told her to return the book to me. Then, to make matters worse, Daddy came in and said something critical, also. Anne, predictably offended, flounced out of the room in dramatic fashion, leaving us to wallow in the gloomy wake she left behind.

She probably returned to her diary and wrote about how Daddy and Mummy favour me. (If this were true, why don't I feel that way?) And how they consider me the pretty one and the smart one. And how angry she is at them for always asking her to act more as I do. I wish she would stop complaining about that. And I wish she would stop teasing me about being a "model child" — I don't strive to be a model child, it's just the way I am.

WEDNESDAY, NOVEMBER 11, 1942

British and American troops have landed in Africa. This most welcome news, combined with the Russians' valiant stand at Stalingrad, has filled our hearts with hope.

Prime Minister Churchill said: "This is not the end. It is not even the beginning of the end. But it is, perhaps, the end of the beginning."

I think he is saying that it is going to take longer than we think. But the problem is, I don't know how much longer we have.

FRIDAY, NOVEMBER 13, 1942

It seems that Mr Pfeffer is going to join us in hiding. He wants to wait a week because the Christian dentist he secretly works with still owes him some money and he wants to collect it. There was a long discussion about this and it was decided he has to be here by a week from tomorrow or that's that.

The plan, if he does come, is for him to go to the post office and wait there. Mr Kleiman will then come by, bump into him, and lead him here — Mr Pfeffer following a few discreet feet behind.

He is going to sleep in our room and I will move in with Daddy and Mummy. Having Mr Pfeffer join us is going to put an additional burden on all of us, especially Anne, who has to share a room with him. But Daddy is right, the situation in Holland is worsening each day and we all must sacrifice so one more person can be saved.

As Dickens so eloquently puts it: "The common wretches were left to get out of their difficulties as they could."

MONDAY, NOVEMBER 16, 1942

Peter spends most of the day in his room with his cat, presumably sleeping. I must admit that he is handy at fixing things — he put up padding where we all hit our heads when we go downstairs. Also he seems to do his chores reliably, lugging the sacks of beans up from downstairs, getting the potatoes from the attic, chopping wood, and checking that everything's locked up downstairs at night.

The rest of the time he complains about one illness or the other, both real and imagined, and even wears a scarf to protect his neck from chills.

THURSDAY, NOVEMBER 19, 1942

Mr Pfeffer was quite stunned to see us, thinking, as Daddy had planned, that we had all gone off to safety in Switzerland.

We were gathered upstairs around the dining room table, waiting with coffee and cognac. At first he thought that something must have gone wrong with our plans. He was duly impressed by our audacious hiding place.

Mr Pfeffer said that he has been so frightened recently that he has been staying with various acquaintances at night rather than returning to his apartment.

His stories about the situation in Holland sounded so bad that now I think that maybe Anne is right. Maybe we are lucky to be here. (As always, whenever anyone tells us about what is happening, Mummy and Mrs van Pels cannot hold back the tears. I do but it's not easy.)

So many kids my age have been taken away that the graduating classes at the Jewish schools have been reduced to a frightening degree. At one graduation ceremony a senior appealed to her teachers and parents in the audience for guidance. What should she do if she received a call-up notice as I had? No one had any answers for her. At another graduation a boy was taken directly from the ceremony and put into hiding by his nearly panicked parents.

The Jewish Council makes the situation even worse with their "exemptions", which means you won't be on the list for the call-ups. Naturally they are coveted by everyone. But people suspect the Jewish Council is corrupt. They give the "exemptions" to their friends, relatives, and those who can pay for them.

German military vehicles go from street to street in search of Jews. People sit in darkened rooms night after night, their bags packed, shaking with fear, wondering if it will be the last night they will sleep in their own beds. If tonight will be the night they are dragged away to some Godforsaken place. They sit and listen intently for the sound of vehicles stopping in front of their apartment, of doorbells ringing, of steps running up the stairs.

They dread waking in the morning and seeing who in the neighbourhood is left. They watch helplessly as the moving vans remove the furniture from the homes of those taken away during the night. Furniture to be sent back to Germany for use by German citizens. Christian German citizens.

There are stories of mothers cradling babies in their arms and jumping off the backs of the trucks, running crazily from apartment building to apartment building, desperately looking for Jewish names on the mailboxes, hoping that whoever answers will be kind enough and brave enough to let them in.

People are being dragged out of old-age homes and there are rumours — hideous, bizarre, unbelievable rumours — that Jewish children, younger than me, are being murdered by poison gas.

Mr Pfeffer has so many questions and he never asks only once. What is the procedure and schedule for the bathroom? What are the rules about noise? He appears to be in shock, and who can blame him?

FRIDAY, NOVEMBER 20, 1942

Mummy lights Sabbath candles while Mr Pfeffer leads us in prayer.

SATURDAY, NOVEMBER 28, 1942

We have exceeded our electricity ration and will have to be more careful in the future. Now it is too dark to read after four-thirty.

Another stone added to our already heavy load.

FRIDAY, DECEMBER 4, 1942

Mr Pfeffer and Anne don't seem to be getting along well at all. I don't know who is at fault but Anne is right about one thing: he does have a tendency to make tediously long, sanctimonious speeches.

MONDAY, DECEMBER 7, 1942

We celebrated Chanuka and Saint Nicholas's Day jointly as they fell so very close together this year. We lit candles and gave one another presents: flowers, chocolate, cigarettes (guess who), more chocolates and sewing boxes.

THURSDAY, DECEMBER 10, 1942

Mr van Pels is making sausages and some of them have to dry out so they are hung all around the dining room, which adds a note of pathetic humour to our otherwise humourless environment.


FRIDAY, DECEMBER 11, 1942

Mrs van Pels was Mr Pfeffer's first patient here and quite an impatient (and noisy) one she was. He had to use cologne instead of the proper disinfectant and Vaseline instead of wax.


SATURDAY, DECEMBER 12, 1942

Peeling potatoes while Mummy irons.
Bratwurst and sauerkraut for dinner.


SUNDAY, DECEMBER 13, 1942

Yesterday we had a nice warm bath downstairs in the front office. Anne and I talked about the street urchins — as she so accurately calls them — who roam around the neighbourhood. Like characters out of one of Daddy's Dickens stories, they don't have the proper clothing and are so hungry they eat scraps of food off the street. Some, the bolder ones I would imagine (though maybe they are just the hungrier, more desperate ones), stop people walking by and beg for food.

TUESDAY, DECEMBER 22, 1942

Mr Pfeffer and my sister are certainly having their difficulties. He objects to Anne's talking so much and is constantly shushing her. He might as well object to the ocean having waves. He gets up early to do his arm-flapping exercises (as Anne describes them) and wakes her up, even on Sunday mornings. She says he is driving her absolutely mad.

TUESDAY, JANUARY 5, 1943

Anne had another fight with Mrs van Pels. I don't know why Anne doesn't just ignore her. As Mummy so succinctly puts it, Mrs van Pels is just too stupid to argue with.

WEDNESDAY, JANUARY 6, 1943

I have a constant headache that I am unable to rid myself of.

WEDNESDAY, JANUARY 13, 1943

Every night British bombers fly directly overhead on their way to destroying German cities. Although our spirits are lifted by this, sleeping through the night is becoming an impossibility. The piercing sound of the air-raid sirens begins just as soon as the planes cross the coastline. This is invariably followed by machine-gun and anti-aircraft fire. Sometimes there are even midair battles between British and German planes — they are so near we can actually hear the engines' drone.

We are all worried that one of the bombs might fall near us and start a fire. This old wooden building would go up in a minute and then we would have to run out into the street. We have bags packed just in case, but everyone hopes it won't come to that.

Most nights Anne is so frightened that she comes in and gets into bed with Daddy or lies down on the floor next to him, wrapped up cocoonlike in her blankets (sometimes she's so frightened she won't go to the bathroom until she hears that he is going). She says she feels safe and protected being near him. If only that were true. If only being near Daddy could truly protect us from all of this.

The other night Anne wanted to light a candle because the utter darkness in here makes all of this just that much worse. Daddy wouldn't allow it because it is too risky — what if someone saw there was a light on? But Mummy came to Anne's defence, lighting the candle herself and telling Daddy Anne was not, like him, a veteran soldier.

MONDAY, JANUARY 18, 1943

Daddy is endlessly inventive. He has created a file card system whereby we make note of all the books we read. The information includes title, author, publisher, date read, etc, etc. We treat each book we get as a precious commodity to be passed from person to person. We discuss them endlessly to pass the time, but I would much rather read a book than talk about it. Currently I am reading Goethe's *The Sorrows of Young Werther*, which I find most enjoyable, although slow going.

WEDNESDAY, FEBRUARY 3, 1943

Mr van Pels is *still* complaining about my eating habits. This despite no one, including his wife, paying any attention to him. He thinks I'm trying to maintain my figure. He doesn't see how ludicrous it is: as if having an appetite, living the way we do, is normal and not having one is abnormal. I simply try to eat healthy things like fruits and vegetables, not that I tell him that. Indeed it isn't any of his business, so I simply don't respond to him.

Fortunately Mummy couldn't stand his diatribe one more second and snapped at him, putting an instant end to it. Mrs van Pels turned beet red when Mummy intervened, although I'm not sure if it was because she was embarrassed by her husband or angry with Mummy.

THURSDAY, FEBRUARY 11, 1943

In my estimation all the petty quarrels that are always taking place between one resident or the other (present company excluded) are the result of living in such close proximity. There is absolutely no privacy here — something you take for granted until you have it taken away from you.

TUESDAY, FEBRUARY 16, 1943

The most disappointing birthday of my life and the less said about it the better.

MONDAY, FEBRUARY 22, 1943

Mr and Mrs van Pels are the opposite of Daddy and Mummy. Daddy and Mummy are so civilised and discreet when they disagree. But the van Pelses don't care what they say to each other or who hears it.

WEDNESDAY, FEBRUARY 24, 1943

That clock is driving me crazy.

THURSDAY, FEBRUARY 25, 1943

The van Pelses have been arguing in the most frightful fashion, screaming wretched things at each other, stamping their feet (not during business hours, of course); neither one listening to a word the other is saying (not that either one is saying anything worthwhile).

Sometimes Daddy and Mummy listen intently to the

argument, trying to judge whether or not it is becoming so bad that they will have to intervene.

After the storm has blown over they have these lovey-dovey reconciliations, complete with cute nicknames. (Kerli is his for her and Putti is hers for him.) It's absolutely nauseating. If you ask me it's no mystery why Peter is as forlorn and lost as he is.

FRIDAY, MARCH 5, 1943

Reading Heine:

How love and faith and humour
Had disappeared from the earth,
How the price of coffee had risen,
And how little a mark was worth.

Gone are the childish pretendings,
And everything else rolls past,
Money and world and eras,
And faith and love and trust.

TUESDAY, MARCH 9, 1943

When Anne feels blue she sometimes takes to wandering from room to room, like a ghost in that ghastly nightdress she insists on wearing. Other times she just sleeps most of the day.

I think Anne's exuberant personality helps her hide from her fears — fears about what will become of us. Her bravery is formidable but is being sorely tested here.

That's one of the differences between us — I don't pretend not to be scared.

MONDAY, MARCH 15, 1943

Shadow kisses, shadow bliss,
Shadow life, forever gay!
Do you think, dear foolishness,
Everything is here to stay?

What we lovingly possessed,
Fades away like reverie;
Hearts grow heedless in the breast,
Eyes forget to see.

— Heine

TUESDAY, MARCH 23, 1943

I had a handsome homeland long ago.
The oak there grew so tall,

91

Meek violets curtsied low.
I dreamed it all.

In German I was kissed, in German heard
(Hard to believe how sweet they seemed)
The words "I love you" then!
It was all dreamed.

— *Heine*

FRIDAY, MARCH 26, 1943

Last night Peter heard someone fiddling with the warehouse door and came and whispered something about it to Daddy. The two of them went downstairs to investigate while I tried to calm down Anne, who was as usual a nervous wreck and white as a sheet (which is not to say I wasn't; I just control it).

As it turned out there was indeed someone down there. We all scurried upstairs and sat quietly for hours, waiting it out, hoping for the best. Mr van Pels had a bad cold and his coughing was making us all nervous. We gave him some codeine that fortunately worked at once. It was quite a while before Daddy came up and reported it was all right.

The shortage of food and the severity of general

92

rationing has resulted in a sharp increase in the number of burglaries in the area. We are tormented by the ever present possibility that someone might break in — looking for something to steal and sell on the black market. They then might hear us and call the police. So many people are eager to collect the reward for turning in Jews in hiding.

We must be more careful. Even something you wouldn't normally think twice about — like leaving the chairs where they are downstairs after listening to the wireless. Even just leaving the wireless tuned to the BBC could mean the end for us if someone breaks in and discovers it.

SATURDAY, MARCH 27, 1943

We have rats, of all things. As if there aren't enough rats around outside, we have to have them inside as well. When Peter went to get some old newspapers he put his hand on the trapdoor leading up to the attic and a rat bit his hand, actually drawing blood.

Peter is going to have his cat sleep there, which will hopefully have an effect.

SUNDAY, MARCH 28, 1943

We listened to Hans Rauter give a speech on the radio. He is the head of the Nazi police. He said that all Jews have to be out of Germany and any of the countries currently occupied by July 1.

It's hard to believe that all this is really happening. That people are actually able to convince themselves that there is someone who is the cause of all their trouble. That all they have to do is rid themselves of these people — these Jewish people — and all their worries and woes will vanish into thin air. As if life could be that simple.

### THURSDAY, APRIL 1, 1943

There was an important business meeting downstairs and Daddy was very concerned about how it would turn out. He is frustrated that he is unable to run the business the way he has in the past. He wanted me to help him lie on the floor and listen. The meeting went on all morning and into the afternoon, by which time poor Daddy could hardly straighten up. Anne took his place but fell asleep. Fortunately I was able to report fully to Daddy all that he had missed.

### FRIDAY, APRIL 2, 1943

Anne is so mean to Mummy sometimes. Usually Daddy goes to her at night but this time Mummy went because

Daddy was busy. She offered to say her prayers with Anne but she declined Mummy's gracious offer.

Mummy was crying when she returned to our room. "Love cannot be forced," she said, looking sad and stricken. She has dark rings under her eyes from lack of sleep and worries all the time. She sees no end to our plight and believes that the outlook is bleak.

Daddy tries to get her to think more positively, to take heart that the Allies are coming to save us, and to have more faith in the future, but I think Mummy resents his constant prodding.

She likes to talk to Miep, which I think helps. Even though Miep is incredibly busy when she comes up in the mornings she always takes time to listen to Mummy's worries, which helps relieve her burdens.

FRIDAY, APRIL 16, 1943

Anne thinks she is the only girl in the world who has ever suffered from being misunderstood; who has ever thought about her parents, friendship, loneliness, or the difficulties of finding someone to love for the rest of your life.

WEDNESDAY, APRIL 21, 1943

Listening to, or rather, should I say, sitting through, the dinner-table conversation tonight I thought about how much I missed listening to Mr Goslar talk about Palestine. I so long to talk again with my Zionist friends about our plans for settling there and building a better world

MONDAY, MAY 3, 1943

All our clothes are the worse for wear. Daddy's trousers are frayed and his tie is dirty — I've never seen him look like this. Anne's shoes don't fit, she can't button some of her shirts, and her vests no longer fit around her not-so-skinny body. My bras are too small.

TUESDAY, MAY 11, 1943

Mr van Pels thinks we might have to remain here until the end of the year, which is more than I can bear thinking about right now.

Sometimes I think Mummy is right and the war will go on and on and we will all grow old here.

TUESDAY, JUNE 1, 1943

The food situation here is dire. For two weeks we have had boiled lettuce and tasteless potatoes. We have to rely on tinned foods: vegetables, fish, fruit, etc., etc. Daddy was so wise to think of stocking up on these items months before we went into hiding.

SATURDAY, JUNE 12, 1943

Anne's fourteenth birthday.

WEDNESDAY, JUNE 16, 1943

Nerves are on edge and tempers short. I remain aloof from all these petty arguments but am still saddened by them.

SUNDAY, JUNE 20, 1943

Anne says sharing a room with Mr Pfeffer is horrible. He is completely out of sorts if he doesn't get his afternoon nap; continues to wake her early, even on Sunday mornings, because he insists on doing his exercises then; and spends an incredible amount of time in the bathroom. When she tries to go to sleep he tosses and turns fitfully and sounds like he is constantly gasping for breath. Besides that he snores *terribly*.

I can't judge these things because I haven't witnessed them firsthand. She's right, however, about his table manners, which are wanting, to say the least. He serves himself first and foremost (and the most) and seems totally unconcerned about how much is left for the rest of us.

WEDNESDAY, JUNE 23, 1943

Mr Kleiman has obtained ration cards on the black market for us. Now we can get much needed items like clothes, medicine, etc, etc.

MONDAY, JULY 5, 1943

We have been here a year.

SUNDAY, JULY 11, 1943

Anne is having trouble with her eyes and might need glasses. Being trapped in here makes that somewhat complicated, to say the least. Mummy has been considering having her go with someone to the optician's. Naturally Anne was petrified by the idea. In the end it was decided that we simply can't risk it.

TUESDAY, JULY 13, 1943

The British have landed in Sicily, and Daddy says he has high hopes for a quick finish. We can't listen on the big radio downstairs any more because it had to be turned in to the authorities. We have a little one up here that we can listen to, though.

Anne and Mr Pfeffer have been arguing for days about the little table in their room. Anne likes to spend as much time as she can there. Sometimes she writes in Daddy's room and sometimes downstairs. But she can't write at the dining-room table upstairs. There's simply too much commotion there and too many people with too much time on their hands.

It's really admirable how diligent she is about her diary. Although I find writing in mine comforting and illuminating I can't be bothered to record something each day and at such length as Anne does. Especially in view of how little actually happens here, at least as far as I'm concerned. But for my sister it's all one long, melodramatic movie, and each squabble and every quarrel is grist for her busy little mill.

Holding her fountain pen in that odd little grip she invented after she sprained her thumb, she spends countless hours agonising over every word, updating every entry, constantly revising and rewriting. It's almost as if she truly

99

expects that someday millions of people will be reading her diary. As if she really believes that some day she is going to become a world-famous writer. Well, at least it keeps her mind occupied.

Currently Anne is allowed to use the table from 2.30 to 4.00, which is when Mr Pfeffer takes his afternoon nap. But she would like to use it more. Much to her credit she has tried to talk to Mr Pfeffer, but he won't even condescend to discuss it with her. He claims he needs the desk for his own work that he considers infinitely more important than Anne's "childish scribblings".

Daddy defended Anne's writing, explaining that although it might seem trifling to Mr Pfeffer it wasn't to Anne. Ever the diplomat, Daddy was able to work out a compromise. Anne will work at the table until five o'clock two afternoons and on weekends.

She and Mr Pfeffer are not presently speaking.

FRIDAY, JULY 16, 1943

There was another burglary downstairs. They broke through the warehouse door with a crowbar or some such thing. They took some money from the cashboxes and our precious ration coupons.

MONDAY, JULY 19, 1943

Helping Bep with her office work (keeping the checking accounts up to date; filing correspondence; writing up invoices; maintaining the salesbook, etc, etc), although tedious, makes me at least feel useful. Also, in some small way, I feel I am repaying her for her kindness.

They are all such angels: Mr Kugler, Mr Kleiman, Miep, and Bep. Bep is in and out and up and down all day getting small things for us. Day after day Miep comes and gets the shopping list. She then has to wait in line for hours and be sure to shop at various stores so no one will be able to tell she is shopping for eight in hiding. Somehow she manages to do everything competently and cheerfully. As if that wasn't enough she brings us books from the library on Saturdays, which I truly look forward to. I can survive without much food or water but I need to read.


FRIDAY, JULY 23, 1943

I told Anne I was thinking of signing up for a calligraphy course that is being offered by the same company that sent us the shorthand course. This managed, somehow, to become yet another argument between her and

Mummy. Anne wants to take the course but Mummy won't allow it because of Anne's worsening eyesight. She does spend a lot of time reading Greek and Roman mythology, doing family trees, and reading in general and, of course, writing in her diary every chance she gets. Mummy is afraid that taking the calligraphy course will be just too much for her.

SATURDAY, JULY 24, 1943

Anne took a survey about what was the first thing everyone was going to do "after the war". I agreed with Mr van Pels about the long hot bath; Mrs van Pels longs for some good pastries; Peter a film; Mr Pfeffer to see his wife; Daddy only wants to visit Bep's father; and Mummy wants a really good cup of coffee. Anne couldn't be pinned down to one thing. I think she just wants to be home, as we all do.

MONDAY, JULY 26, 1943

Air-raid sirens, shooting, and bombs falling all day long. It was so bad the house was shaking. The smoke from the nearby fires was so thick you could smell it and it turned the air grey. This continued through dinnertime, and we could hear the dreadful droning of the engines as the planes flew right above us.

## TUESDAY, AUGUST 3, 1943

The van Pelses have been arguing all week. Mrs van Pels cries every time she hears an air-raid siren.

## TUESDAY, AUGUST 10, 1943

That awful clock has been silenced. The Germans need to melt down the bells for the war effort.

## WEDNESDAY, AUGUST 11, 1943

The weather has been bad lately so there are no British bombers flying overhead and hence no air-raid sirens. Of course, this is a mixed blessing. The peace and quiet at night is welcome but the most important thing is that the war come to an end at the soonest possible date.

## WEDNESDAY, SEPTEMBER 1, 1943

Sometimes at night, after the workers have all gone home and there is no one downstairs, the telephone rings. It rings and rings, and, of course, since there is no one down there, it goes unanswered. And sometimes the doorbell is rung as well. We never know who it is. It could be some of the kids in the neighbourhood who seem to roam around at all hours or it could be the police.

Each night here is eerie in its own way.

THURSDAY, SEPTEMBER 9, 1943

Italy has surrendered to the Allies. We just heard the news on the radio. Maybe Daddy is right and this horrible war will be over soon.

THURSDAY, SEPTEMBER 16, 1943

Things are deteriorating here by the minute. There are so many individual quarrels and resentments spoken and unspoken that hardly anyone speaks at dinner.

Daddy has become tired of constantly negotiating truces between the always warring parties (present company excluded).

Anne's right; we have all forgotten how to laugh. But what is there to laugh about?

MONDAY, SEPTEMBER 20, 1943

Daddy measured our growth this morning. Anne is getting quite tall.

WEDNESDAY, SEPTEMBER 22, 1943

On top of our endless list of worries we can now add one more. Mr van Maaren, who works in the warehouse, is acting suspiciously, according to Mr Kugler and Miep. Although he appears to be a good worker he's always snooping around and asking questions about things that shouldn't concern him. Mr Kugler found him one day scraping the blue tinting off the windows that overlook the entrance to our annexe. Mr Kugler had put it there for the express purpose of obscuring the view. When Mr van Maaren is around our friends in the office are on their guard and especially cautious about coming up here for fear he will follow them.

No one trusts him but they are afraid to just dismiss him because he might then call the police.

FRIDAY, OCTOBER 29, 1943

Mr and Mrs van Pels are arguing over money again. The situation has been quite serious ever since Mr van Pels lost his wallet and all the money in it one night when he was downstairs in the warehouse. Of course, now we all have to wonder who the thief is and does he know about us. They can't find a buyer for Peter's bicycle or for Mr van Pels's suit, so Mrs van Pels's clothes — her fur coats, dresses, shoes, hats, etc — are the only alternative.

Mr van Pels finally persuaded his reluctant wife to sell her precious rabbit-skin coat to a furrier that Mr Kleiman knows. Mr Kleiman got them a good price for it, but now they are arguing about what to do with the money. Mrs van Pels wants to save the money until "after the war" when she can, once again, buy nice clothes for her wardrobe. Mr van Pels insists they need it now for household expenses — meaning, I think, cigarettes.

After much histrionics (yelling, screaming, foot stomping, and weeping constant tears), Mr van Pels prevailed.

SATURDAY, OCTOBER 30, 1943

Anne doesn't look well and we are all worried about her. She has always been frail and susceptible to any number of recurring illnesses. Mmmy is constantly feeling her forehead to see if she has a fever and inquiring about her bowel movements. Mummy is also concerned that she is taking her valerian every day. Of course living here is certainly not good for anyone's health, mental or physical, least of all my sister's.

## THURSDAY, NOVEMBER 4, 1943

Daddy insisted that I sign up for a Latin course with him. Honestly I'm not up to doing much of anything lately, but I have to admit that working on the Latin with Daddy helps pass the time.

## MONDAY, NOVEMBER 15, 1943

Anne is upset because her favourite fountain pen — the one Grandmother gave her when she was nine and the only one she uses to write in her diary — was accidentally destroyed.

She must have left it on the table when she was writing in her diary. Daddy and I needed the table to do our Latin and so Anne occupied herself rubbing the mould off the beans so they could be cooked and eaten without making us sick. She seemed quite annoyed when Daddy and I arrived and must have left the pen on the table because the pen was cooked in the fire with the beans. Daddy found the clip of the pen, which was all that remained, in the stove.

## SUNDAY, NOVEMBER 21, 1943

Mr Pfeffer continues to complain to anyone who will listen that no one here likes him. (He does have a valid point.) He and Mr van Pels are not currently speaking to each other, although no one knows precisely why. Of course the fact that Mr Pfeffer refers to Mrs van Pels as a not-too-intelligent female bovine and that Mrs van Pels returns the favour by referring to his "finicky" nature might have something to do with it.

FRIDAY, NOVEMBER 26, 1943

My corrected Latin lessons came back and my correspondence teacher (who, of course, doesn't know my real name — she thinks I'm Bep Voskuijl) said that I was doing quite nicely.

SUNDAY, NOVEMBER 28, 1943

Anne was deeply troubled by a dream she had two nights ago. It was about Lies. Anne saw her in one of those horrible camps we have been hearing about. She looked pale and tired and was dressed in rags. She was hurt that Anne had left her to this cruel fate while she was safe, here, in our hiding place.

The dream disturbed Anne greatly. She talked, jumping from one topic to the next, about right and wrong and life and death. She said that sometimes she was so scared she just wanted to scream out loud. She says that she is losing what little faith she had in God.

108

I didn't really know what to say to her. Anne and I hardly talk these days, something I feel badly about. I wish I could bridge the distance that seems to be growing between us. I feel it is my responsibility since I am the older sister but it is difficult to talk to Anne sometimes.

Unlike my sister I try not to dwell on things like God. Of course maybe the reason I don't like to think about it is I don't want to admit that my faith is so precarious that under pressure — living as we all do now with the evil that surrounds us — I will abandon hope.

I'm not sure how I feel.

I just try to get from day to day without falling into the abyss.


WEDNESDAY, DECEMBER 1, 1943

There is only one solution to all of this: we Jews need our own homeland. A place of refuge that is ours, where we don't have to worry about fitting in or about being approved of. A place where we will no longer be the minority, tolerated when times are good and persecuted when a handy scapegoat is needed.

We will never be safe and secure until we are the majority and can dictate our own destiny.

We can no longer hope to be assimilated into the population at large, no matter what country we are born in: Germany, Britain, France, or America. It is not only Germany where hatred for Jews resides.

Daddy, I know, would never agree with me about this. His German heritage is too dear to him. But look at what has happened. He was wounded in the First World War fighting for his country; became an honest, hardworking businessman; raised a family and taught his children to know and appreciate all that is fine and good in German culture. He and Mummy have always considered themselves Germans first and foremost. Now, in an instant, they have become outcasts. Driven from their homes, forced to pack up all their possessions and flee. Only to be hounded wherever they go.

How right and prophetic Herzl was. Right that "We are a people. One people." And prophetic that, indeed, the time has come.

I only wonder if it is too late, not only for me, but for all of us.

WEDNESDAY, DECEMBER 15, 1943

I had a dream about Palestine.

It was just as I imagined it would be. Everyone was my

age and we were all working together untiringly and unselfishly. We were all pioneers in uncharted territory. Living communally, sharing everything. A whole different way of looking at life.

All my people, Jewish people. Every one of us utterly devoted to the higher cause of building a Jewish state.

I want to believe that Palestine is not just a utopian dream but a vision that can be realised.

WEDNESDAY, DECEMBER 22, 1943

Anne has a bad cold. She has to stifle the noise of her coughing by crawling under the blankets. Mummy plies her with one remedy after another: grape sugar, cod liver oil, calcium, milk and honey, hot and cold compresses, gargling, hot water bottles, etc, etc; ad infinitum, ad nauseam.

SUNDAY, DECEMBER 26, 1943

We are closing out the year with yet more petty arguments and bickering. Recent topics of contention are which pots and pans to use and when, how to peel potatoes, and whether or not meat should have any fat on it.

Sometimes I think we should have gone into hiding with the Goslars. At least their babies were real babies. Grown-up babies is what we have here.

TUESDAY, DECEMBER 28, 1943

Miep made a Christmas cake with "Peace 1944" on it. We can only hope.

WEDNESDAY, JANUARY 5, 1944

Anne seems so distant and distracted.

She asked me about the oddest thing. She wanted to know if I remembered the time Mummy and I took her for her dentist appointment and she rode her bicycle. After the dentist we two decided to go shopping but Mummy wouldn't let Anne go because of the bicycle, which Mummy wanted her to take right home.

She wanted to know if I remembered laughing at her, along with Mummy, despite her sobbing. She told me that when our backs were turned she stuck her tongue out at us.

I remembered it vaguely, but Anne remembered it with the utmost clarity, as if it happened yesterday.

TUESDAY, JANUARY 11, 1944

We have too much time on our hands. Too much time to ponder, dwell, and obsess about our circumstances and idiosyncrasies. We suffer without the daily distractions we took for granted: school, work, friends, sports, social activities, holidays — the common comings and goings of the ordinary day. All the things that keep you active and occupied and prevent you from becoming insular and introspective in the extreme. All the things that keep you sane.

WEDNESDAY, JANUARY 12, 1944

Anne is, I think, developing quite a little crush on Peter van Pels. Frankly I don't think he can hold a candle to Hello but he is, shall we say, "eligible". Lately Anne has been helping him with his crossword puzzles, which appear truly to puzzle him.

THURSDAY, JANUARY 13, 1944

Anne's latest obsession is ballet, which she has been practising practically every night. She's even made her own dance outfit — at least I think that's what it is. It formerly functioned as one of Mummy's slips. Her attempt to convert her gym shoes to ballet shoes was not quite as successful.

Last night she placed a cushion on the floor and held the heel of her foot while extending her leg — quite a feat.

SUNDAY, JANUARY 16, 1944

Mummy's birthday. The office staff presented her with a mocha cake made from hard-to-get pre-war ingredients.

She fully enjoyed it — both the sentiment behind it and the cake itself.

Her birthday wish is to never see the van Pelses again for the rest of her life. They certainly are a trial.

FRIDAY, JANUARY 21, 1944

Mr Gies and Mr Kleiman talked about the heroic efforts of the Dutch underground. How they forge ID cards, get ration coupons, and steal registration cards from the files the Germans compiled so that the person no longer officially exists and, therefore, won't be taken away.

They risk their lives daily, telling one another as little as possible about their activities so that if they are caught they will not, indeed cannot, betray one another. They seek out priests who sometimes are willing to provide the names of good Christian families who offer to shelter Jewish children.

Then they try to find Jewish parents willing to place, for safety's sake, their precious children with these Christian families. They told how extraordinarily difficult it was for them, watching as the parents agonised over their decision, weighing one impossible choice against another. Should they put their children into the arms of strangers, no matter how well-meaning they were? Will this ensure that their children will survive? Does this mean that they will never see them again?

They told how difficult it was for them to watch the families cry as they turned their children over. Most, however, refused, believing as we did that the family had to remain together.

And the pain doesn't even end there. Once placed, the child might not be a good fit with the foster family or might accidentally betray himself. The neighbours might become suspicious. There are people all over Holland now eager to report Jewish children to the authorities and collect the reward. And so the children might have to be moved again and again.

There were times when they resorted to simply snatching children off the backs of German military trucks during a roundup.

One story was truly heartbreaking. A member of the underground was trying to persuade the parents of a young boy to let him take the child into hiding with a Christian family. The parents wanted to think about it overnight. When the underground worker returned the next day the entire family had been taken away.

MONDAY, JANUARY 24, 1944

Our dinner-table conversation is less than stimulating. Most of the time we talk about how wonderful the meal is, a conversation which varies in length and intensity in inverse proportion to the actual quality of the meal.

Then all the adults (except for Daddy) tell unfunny jokes and boring stories that we've all heard so many times before that we can't wait till they end.

One wonders if Mr Pfeffer really thinks any of us are interested in hearing how he learned to swim at the precocious (this is, I think, the point of this otherwise pointless story) age of four or the details of his wife's carefully chosen, expensive, and extensive wardrobe.

TUESDAY, JANUARY 25, 1944

The silly conversation we (Anne, Peter, and I) had a couple of days ago about the unknown gender of Peter's cat still brings a smile to my face. Anne and Peter are some combination: he's incredibly naive and my sister's fearless to a fault.

Lately sex seems to be her favourite topic, and I don't even want to speculate about what she and Peter are doing when they are together. They excused themselves so that they could have a closer examination and determine, with medical certainty, the cat's gender.

I stayed behind and finished peeling the potatoes.


SATURDAY, FEBRUARY 5, 1944

There are reports in the newspapers of a possible British invasion of Holland. This is, of course, the most welcome news. However (there always seems to be a however these days), there are grave complications to consider if and when it comes.

For one thing, British bombs might strike us and we might perish from a direct hit or from the fire caused by one that falls nearby.

Secondly, the Germans have said that they will do everything in their power to repel a British invasion, but if forced to withdraw, they will take the entire population with them. As absurd as that sounds, if we have learned anything in the past ten years it is that the Germans are capable of the most horrendous acts.

And there's more.

There are reports that the Germans will flood the entire country if the British invade. There are even maps showing which parts of Holland will then be underwater.

What would we do if the water from the canal right outside our door started to rise? Would the building collapse, since it's already wobbly and leans to one side even now? Would we have to abandon the building?

Anne thought the macabre turn the conversation then took was quite humorous: for example, Peter doesn't know how to swim; Mrs van Pels doesn't have her bathing suit; should we get a small boat, etc, etc. Good material for her diary, I should think.

For me I find no humour in the situation.

TUESDAY, FEBRUARY 8, 1944

We have sunk so low that now a mere pin can cause an argument.

Two nights ago I was pulling the bedcover over me and a pin Mummy had left in a patch she had sewn stuck me. Daddy said something about Mummy's being too careless, which, although true lately, was all Anne needed. When Mummy came in Anne was quite mean to her, nearly accusing her of purposely leaving the pin in the patch, which was a foolish thing to say — Mummy would never do anything like that.

Mummy, visibly irritated, accused Anne of being sloppy herself, although some of the examples Mummy was pointing to were my things, which I admitted to but which did little good as the two of them are just constantly at each other's throats.

WEDNESDAY, FEBRUARY 9, 1944

Anne seems lost and listless lately, wandering once again from room to room, unable to concentrate on anything for more than a minute and never reading more than a paragraph at a time. She looks as if she's been crying again.

MONDAY, FEBRUARY 14, 1944

We were listening to music on the small wireless and Mr Pfeffer was feebly fiddling with the dials in a futile attempt to improve the already quite satisfactory quality of the reception.

Understandably Peter lost patience with the whole thing and asked Mr Pfeffer if it were possible that he might stop playing with the dials anytime soon.

I've never seen Peter look that angry, not even when his parents are picking on him (although he is more feisty lately than when we first came here, but then again all of us are). Mr Pfeffer replied, in his typical condescending way, that he was trying to get it "just so". When Mr van Pels joined in the fray on his son's side Mr Pfeffer was forced to retreat and lick his wounds.

Mr Pfeffer later told Mummy that Peter had apologised to him and he had graciously accepted. But, as it turns out, Peter did no such thing, and he and Mr Pfeffer are not currently speaking.


WEDNESDAY, FEBRUARY 16, 1944

Another dismal birthday.

I'm eighteen.


TUESDAY, FEBRUARY 22, 1944

I think Anne's flirtation with Peter van Pels is escalating and becoming mutual. They both pretend not to be looking at each other throughout dinner, which is mildly amusing. And they spend a great deal of time in either his room or the attic. Anne says she likes to feel the sun and breathe the fresh air from the open window, look out at the chestnut tree and the blue sky with the seagulls floating by. She said it makes her happy, if only for the moment.

Frankly I don't think it's making Mummy too happy.

WEDNESDAY, FEBRUARY 23, 1944

The longer we remain in hiding, the more I think I will simply grow old here.

SATURDAY, FEBRUARY 26, 1944

Anne read part of one of her stories, the one she calls "Eva's Dream". It was quite good, although fragmented.

WEDNESDAY, MARCH 1, 1944

There has been another burglary downstairs.

Mr van Pels discovered that the door leading to Mr Kugler's office was open and the main office was in disarray, as if someone was looking for something. The projector and some important papers are missing.

Since the lock wasn't broken, everyone suspects an inside job, meaning Mr van Maaren.

The burglar must have been startled by Mr van Pels's entry and then ran. But this means that the burglar knows that someone was in the building, besides him, after hours. Hopefully it was just a common thief. If not, if it was Mr van Maaren or someone else who now suspects our presence, then our lives are truly in danger.

We have little choice but to wait and hope.

Fear is our constant companion.

More arguments as everyone seems terribly irritable.

While we were cleaning up the kitchen (I hope some-day not to have to wash another dish or scrub another pan), Bep admitted that she was not very hopeful about the future. Mummy, who was trying to make her be positive, said she should think about all the people who had it worse than she did.

Anne immediately jumped on Mummy, criticising what she said to Bep. Mummy told Anne she should keep her thoughts to herself, something I'm sure Anne will never do.

Then Daddy got annoyed, which of course sent Anne completely over the edge.

I tried to calm her down, with little success. Anne personifies the scientific dictum that bodies at rest tend to stay at rest and bodies in motion tend to stay in motion, especially her lips. Being quiet is not a natural state for her.

I don't think she realises how impertinent she can be sometimes. I don't think that Mummy favours me, it's just that Mummy is so exasperated by her sometimes. And she thinks that Mummy doesn't want her to have her own opinions, but that isn't the case. Mummy just wants Anne to keep them to herself sometimes, especially around other people. Of course, now that we are around other people nearly all the time this is even more difficult for Anne than it was before. I think the situation is harder on her than any of us. We're so confined here that every encounter is a potential spark, every spark a potential flare-up, and every flare-up a potential conflagration.

## SUNDAY, MARCH 12, 1944

Yesterday Anne seemed quite depressed and slept until four in the afternoon. We were all, naturally, very concerned, especially Mummy. I know Anne found all her questions annoying. Mummy is constantly inquiring after Anne's condition, sometimes on an hourly basis. The slightest untoward behaviour by Anne gives rise to oceans of questions and concerns.

Anne put her off with her ubiquitous headache excuse. Anne told me once that sleeping is the only way she can sometimes escape the overwhelming sense of sadness that surrounds us here, so I suspect that was the reason.

## TUESDAY, MARCH 14, 1944

The people from whom we get our ration coupons have been arrested. This is very bad news. We are nearly out of butter and margarine, which means porridge instead of fried potatoes. Mummy spoke yesterday about how dearly she would like a slice of nice, fresh rye bread.

Tonight we had kale that smelled so bad that my most dramatic sister ate with a perfumed handkerchief pressed to her delicate nostrils.

Truthfully I have no appetite.

MONDAY, MARCH 20, 1944

My sister is concerned that, because of her relationship with Peter (which is now in full flower), I will feel left out. Although I think it was thoughtful of her to consider my feelings I assured her that I wasn't in the least bit jealous. Honestly I can't imagine where she would get an idea like that. I haven't said two words to Peter since I've known him. Of course I didn't say anything about my true view of Peter. About what a dullard I think he is. Nor did I say anything about his invitation to join them — an invitation I declined. I tried to tell her tactfully that Peter was not someone I would ever consider having a relationship with.

I mentioned in the kindest way that Peter was more suited intellectually to her. I thought that was the best way to put it. Aside from his numerous shortcomings Peter and

I do not agree about religion. He once told me he would rather have been born a Christian and was going to become one "after the war". I could never care for someone like that.

I found her suggestion that I should look upon Peter as a brother incomprehensible. I offered, so as not to hurt her feelings, that I might possibly develop feelings for Peter someday.

I suggested that she might be misinterpreting my behaviour as jealousy and admitted that in my heart of hearts I did hope someday to find someone of my own. I told her that the type of person I would choose for myself would have to be my intellectual equal and someone who would know me instinctually. Until then I was content to remain the odd one out. Given our present situation this is not about to change.

I assured her there was no reason on earth for her to feel any prick of conscience on my account because she spends so much time with Peter, and she shouldn't for a moment think she is depriving me of anything.

I urged her to enjoy herself as much as possible, having found someone she wishes to spend her time with.

THURSDAY, MARCH 23, 1944

A plane crashed into a school near here yesterday. Fortunately the children were not in it at the time, otherwise the damage would have been even greater. As it was, three people were killed and many more injured in the resulting fire. The Germans shot at the airmen as they parachuted to earth.

SATURDAY, MARCH 25, 1944

Anne is going to Peter's room nearly every night now. Mr and Mrs van Pels don't seem to mind much, but I think Daddy and Mummy are quite concerned.

MONDAY, MARCH 27, 1944

Mr van Pels and Mr Pfeffer tease Anne about spending so much time in Peter's room. "Anne's second home" they call it. I don't know which astounds me more, their immaturity or their insensitivity. My sister has to share a room with a man who is forty years older than she is. A man who, in my opinion, spends half his life writing letters to his wife and having Miep risk her life delivering them. Miep tells Mrs Pfeffer that she doesn't know where he is and I think Mrs Pfeffer is smart enough not to inquire further. Such are the times we live in.

TUESDAY, MARCH 28, 1944

The political debate continues and intensifies as the adults listen to the radio continually. Is the war going well? When will the British invade? Where are the Americans? Of course, what no one says out loud is will we be able to last?


WEDNESDAY, MARCH 29, 1944

Mrs van Pels asked Anne if she could trust the two of them alone in Peter's room. Mummy has told Anne that she doesn't like the way Peter looks at her (Anne, that is) and she has to stop going up to his room so frequently.

It remains to be seen what Anne will do.

My sister is most wilful.


THURSDAY, MARCH 30, 1944

Anne is very excited. Last night on the BBC, Mr Bolkestein, who is the Minister of Education, Art and Science for the Dutch government in exile, made an announcement. They will be asking for those who have been writing letters and keeping diaries to send them to the government at the end of the war so they can document the civilian aspect of the war. So that future generations will know what we have had to endure.

Anne and I will both, of course, comply, but Anne sees this as a great creative opportunity and not, as I do, merely a civic duty.

She's contemplating rewriting everything she's written thus far, quite an undertaking if I understand her correctly. She's thinking of turning her diary into a novel of some sort called *The Secret Annexe*.

MONDAY, APRIL 3, 1944

The food situation deteriorates daily. We can no longer hope to eat a variety of foods and have to be satisfied with whatever we can get. This means that sometimes we eat the same food day after day, for days at a time. Endive, spinach, kohlrabi, cucumbers, tomatoes, sauerkraut, kidney beans, and always potatoes.

WEDNESDAY, APRIL 5, 1944

Miep, Bep, and our other daily visitors try to hide as much as they can from us but each day they contribute different pieces of the puzzle that, when put together, is a Holland I don't recognise.

A Holland where people are cold due to lack of coal; wait in food lines for hours on end; can't leave their cars, even for a moment, because they will be stolen; worry that their homes will be broken into by roving bands of kids looking for something, anything, to sell on the black market; walk around in shabby clothes and worn-out shoes. (Even if you had enough money to take your shoes to the repair shop, it could take as long as four months and by then someone will have stolen them.)

FRIDAY, APRIL 7, 1944

Played Monopoly.

TUESDAY, APRIL 11, 1944

Last Sunday evening Mr Pfeffer discovered that Peter and Anne had used the cushion he uses at night for a pillow to sit on up in the attic and Peter's cat was with them. He fears fleas — a valid fear, but not nearly worth the hysterical fit he threw.

After the tempest in a teapot subsided a real one arose.

At nine-thirty that same night Peter came downstairs, knocked, and asked if Daddy could help him with his English. As Anne pointed out, it was a preposterously transparent excuse. They then got the other two men and went down to investigate while we waited upstairs. We heard nothing for about fifteen minutes then a loud bang.

The men came up and told us to go upstairs to the

van Pelses' room, turn out the lights, and remain absolutely silent because they were expecting the police to come. Without any further explanation they returned downstairs.

A few minutes later they came back up and told us what had transpired. Peter had seen a large plank of wood missing from the warehouse door and, believing that someone was in the process of breaking in, came to get Daddy. When the other two joined them and they went downstairs they did indeed hear something. Mr van Pels instinctively cried out, "Police", which caused the thieves to leave the building.

A couple walked by and shone their flashlight in. It was assumed they would call to report the break-in. Fearing the arrival of the police at any moment, we had to be quiet, which meant, among other things, not using the toilet (we had to resort to using Peter's wastepaper basket). To make matters worse it was Easter Sunday and the offices wouldn't be open until Tuesday so we would have to remain quiet for days.

Although everyone had to whisper, that didn't prevent them from panicking. Mrs van Pels wanted to destroy the radio, and Mr Pfeffer suggested Anne and I burn our diaries. As always I paid no attention to him, and Anne, who nearly had a fit, said that if her diary were to perish then so would she.

Fortunately the conversation went on to other fears, real and imagined. We were all terrified that we were about to be discovered. I trembled at the thought. What would I do? What would I say? What would they do to us?

The police did indeed come and came as close as the other side of the bookcase that hides the entrance to our hiding place. It was my worst moment. Fortunately they came no further and left.

Finally Daddy used the office phone to call Mr Kugler, who in turn told Miep, who came on Monday morning and gave us the all clear. I didn't fully realise the awful state we were in until I saw the look on Miep's face when Anne ran up to her, sobbing, and threw her arms around her.

SATURDAY, APRIL 15, 1944

A number of changes have been made in the wake of the horrible scare last weekend.

For one thing a carpenter is coming to reinforce the warehouse doors. But also we are going to have to be even more careful. No sitting downstairs in the offices at night. Peter has to make his nightly rounds earlier. No using the toilet after nine-thirty.

MONDAY, APRIL 17, 1944

Peter didn't unlock the front door in the morning (it is locked from the inside at night), so no one could get in to work. He said he forgot. Mr Kugler had to go in through a window and was quite disturbed at Peter's forgetfulness.

TUESDAY, APRIL 18, 1944

Gave my most grateful sister part of my chemistry exercise book to use for her diary keeping.

FRIDAY, APRIL 21, 1944

Everyone is even more on edge than usual. Mr van Pels grows more irritable by the day without his cigarettes. Mr Pfeffer never stops telling everyone what he thinks (he's an outcast, no one likes him, etc, etc). Even Daddy looks like he's about to have a temper tantrum.

This is due, in large part, to the recent break-in. But also, I think, because of the incredible length of time we have been here. Almost two years, something none of us would have imagined when we began, not even Daddy. The strain is showing. Everyone gets on everyone's nerves more quickly and more frequently.

TUESDAY, APRIL 25, 1944

Daddy is sounding more optimistic about the course of the war than I've heard him in a while. He expects something big to happen within a month. Mr van Pels disagrees. He says the invasion will never come.

I don't know what to believe.

WEDNESDAY, APRIL 26, 1944

Mr Pfeffer refuses to obey the new, tighter security measures. He continues to go downstairs at night and sit in the office. He got into a heated argument with Daddy and Mr van Pels, and both are barely speaking to him.

Mummy and Mrs van Pels are insisting that he stop giving Miep letters to deliver to his wife. They rightly feel that it is too dangerous to allow it to continue.

THURSDAY, APRIL 27, 1944

We all have bad colds, compliments of my sister. Mrs van Pels complains about the lack of lozenges and tortures us with her horrendous nose-blowing.

TUESDAY, MAY 9, 1944

Daddy and Anne had a long talk about Peter. Daddy said he was disturbed to hear that she was more than friends with him and that he did not approve of anything more intimate than friendship. He said that it was her responsibility to keep the relationship at a distance because boys can be counted on for only one thing, or words to that effect.

He told Anne that he liked Peter but that Peter did not have a strong character and she had to be the strong one. He suggested that she go to Peter's room less frequently.

Anne asked my advice, which I gave her. After that she wrote Daddy a letter, and from the sound of it, she didn't listen to a word I said, which didn't really surprise me.

The letter upset Daddy and he scolded Anne, saying that he and Mummy have always given her all their love, always stood behind her, and they were distressed to read her letter and hear that she seems to feel no responsibility for them.

Anne is now deeply upset and regrets, I think, writing the letter.


THURSDAY, MAY 11, 1944

Mrs van Pels was cutting Peter's hair, as usual (Peter wears swimming trunks and sneakers for the occasion).

They got into an argument about the scissors, and Mrs van Pels hit Peter, which is also not unusual. What was, though, was that Peter hit her back and then grabbed her arm and dragged her across the floor as she protested frantically and to no avail. He let go finally when they reached the base of the stairs leading up to the attic. I must admit that Mrs van Pels's saving grace is that she can laugh at herself, which she proceeded to do, breaking the tension.

She blames the whole thing on our "modern society" that, she claims, teaches children to be rebellious and disrespectful to their parents.

FRIDAY, MAY 12, 1944

Daddy's birthday.

Presents: a decorative box, books, a bottle of beer, and a jar of yogurt, a tie, a pot of syrup, roses, carnations, and spiced gingerbread, which he shared with one and all.

I wrote him a birthday poem, as is our tradition.

THURSDAY, MAY 18, 1944

Listened to Mozart.

SATURDAY, MAY 20, 1944

Anne lost her temper again last night. One of the notebooks that she uses to keep her diary and short stories got soaked when a flower vase got knocked over.

She was near tears before she gave anyone a chance to speak and before she saw that there was no real damage as the wet papers were easily dried.

Her reaction was so extreme and melodramatic that Daddy, Mummy, and I burst out laughing.


THURSDAY, MAY 25, 1944

The police broke into the home of the man we get our vegetables from and discovered the two Jewish people he was giving shelter to. He was, of course, immediately arrested. Besides our obvious concern for him, we now have to eat even less than we were. Since food has been scarce even before, this will take some doing. We will have to forgo breakfast and have porridge for lunch.

Each day we hear more stories about our fellow Jews being found in hiding and taken away.

Where does all this hatred for the Jews come from? As much as we discuss it here and as much as I read, I can't really understand it. Can all of this venom spring from the idea that "we" killed Jesus Christ? I find that difficult to believe. I think people just need someone to blame all their troubles on.

## SATURDAY, MAY 27, 1944

All we talk about lately is the invasion — when will it come, where will it be? Some of us are hopeful, some not so hopeful. I'm afraid I, along with Mummy, fall into the latter category. Daddy and Anne are, of course, optimists. We listen to the radio night after night, hoping for news. Hoping for deliverance.

## WEDNESDAY, MAY 31, 1944

It is unbearably hot in here and impossible to find any relief anywhere in the house. The windows have to remain closed all day, making it absolutely oppressive. Listening to Mrs van Pels's threatening suicide on a daily basis, complaining about her shoes, and lacking clothing suitable for the summer makes being here that much more difficult to bear.

## FRIDAY, JUNE 2, 1944

Anne says she longs for an end to this, no matter what it might be, even if it's bad. She thinks it would have been better, in the long run, if we hadn't gone into hiding.

That way we wouldn't have endangered Miep, Bep, and the others. She says that if we were all dead now the anxiety and torment would be over.

I wish she wouldn't say things like that. She doesn't know what she's saying half the time.

I just want it to be over. I want to go back to the life I had before all this started. Before the Nazis ruined my life.

MONDAY, JUNE 5, 1944

I must give Mr Pfeffer credit, he is most consistent. No matter what is happening he finds something and someone to argue with. His most recent petty squabble involved Daddy and Mummy. The subject: how much butter he is entitled to.

TUESDAY, JUNE 6, 1944

D-day.

The Allies have at long last landed on French soil.

Hundreds of amphibious crafts are landing thousands of troops on the beaches; Allied planes are bombing the coast of France and dropping parachutists.

Prime Minister Churchill and General Eisenhower gave speeches on the radio. The American general, who is the commander of all Allied forces, said that this is the year of victory.

We all hope and pray that this is the real thing.

FRIDAY, JUNE 9, 1944

The Allies are progressing, despite the continued bad weather conditions. British and American troops have engaged the Germans. The radio broadcasts interviews with returning wounded soldiers.

It has been reported that Prime Minister Churchill wanted to land with the troops on D-day but was talked out of it by General Eisenhower.

We all (with the ridiculous exception of Mrs van Pels) have the greatest admiration for Mr Churchill, who, along with President Roosevelt, is doing everything he can to save us.

We must hold on, for the end of our time of trial is nearing.

MONDAY, JUNE 12, 1944

Anne's fifteenth birthday. She received art books, underwear, belts, a handkerchief, and assorted edible treats. I gave her a gold bracelet.

We ought to get an award for how well we have made do here.

WEDNESDAY, JUNE 14, 1944

The Allies are fighting the Germans, pushing them back, liberating French villages as they go.

SATURDAY, JUNE 24, 1944

The invasion continues.

The Russians are relentless and courageous.

We all have our fingers crossed.

TUESDAY, JUNE 27, 1944

Anne has become, I think, obsessed with the subject of sex. She said she thinks it's awful that everyone (and by this she means Daddy, Mummy, and me) always speaks about it in hushed tones and makes it sound so mysterious.

She complains that every time she tries to talk to one of us about it we put her off or, in Mummy's case, tell her to be sure not to talk to boys about it.

She thinks it would be better if parents in general and hers in particular would be more direct about it. She

140

thinks all this stuff about "purity" and "the sanctity of marriage" is all just so much talk and has no place in her world. Her views are quite daring, but not without merit.

SATURDAY, JULY 8, 1944

Strawberries.

Someone Daddy knows from business got them for us. There are so many of them. We clean off the sand and make jam. We have strawberries with everything: porridge, milk, bread.

FRIDAY, JULY 21, 1944

A German general, along with other officers, has attempted to assassinate Adolf Hitler. Unfortunately the plot failed. Reports say that Hitler escaped with only some cuts and burns. The general was shot.

The attempt itself is, however, significant in its own right. If members of the German military see Hitler's madness for what it is, then the German population must also surely see. And surely they are growing tired of this senseless war. They will have only themselves to blame for all that befalls them from here on in.

SATURDAY, JULY 29, 1944

My sister and Peter no longer moon over each other during dinner, and Anne doesn't go up to his room nearly as much as she used to.

Anne says that their differences are coming between them. She also cites his penchant for swearing and talking about trivial matters.

Anne loses interest once she has captured her prey. She enjoys the hunt more than anything else.

MONDAY, JULY 31, 1944

Maybe I will be able to return to school by September.

# PART THREE

# DYING

# Discovery

On the morning of Friday, August 4, 1944, a call came in to Gestapo headquarters. The caller said there were Jews hiding at 263 Prinsengracht. The department chief immediately dispatched SS Oberscharführer Karl Josef Silberbauer to the address.

It was already a warm summer's day. The brilliant sun glinted through the trees that lined the canal, and its rays danced off the water reflecting on to the ceiling of the Opekta offices.

As she did every morning, Miep Gies first went up the stairs to get the shopping list for the day. She and Anne had talked; Anne as always had a thousand questions. Miep couldn't stay — she had to begin her work — but promised to return for a long talk later in the afternoon when she came back with the groceries.

Silberbauer and several Dutch police arrived in a car and parked outside. The doors of the warehouse were open and they entered the building and confronted Victor Kugler. Silberbauer said that he knew Jews were hiding in the building and demanded to be shown the office storerooms.

Kugler, seeing that he had no choice, led them down the hallway towards the front part of the building. Silberbauer ordered Kugler to open the bookcase. Kugler protested that it was only a bookcase but they both knew that Silberbauer knew better. The heavy bookcase, half-filled with worn-out grey file folders, was then yanked open, revealing the narrow stairway.

Kugler, a revolver in his back, led them up the stairs to the hiding place.

It was 10.30 a.m.

Otto Frank was giving Peter an English lesson in the small space just below the attic. Peter was having trouble spelling *double*, which had only one *b*, Otto pointed out.

Otto was startled when he heard someone coming up the stairs. Everyone knew to be quiet at that hour of the morning. Something was very wrong.

Suddenly the door opened and a man with a gun was telling them to raise their hands. They were searched for

146

weapons and taken to the van Pelses' room where the van Pelses and Fritz Pfeffer were being guarded.

Then they were all ordered downstairs.

In the Franks' room Edith and her two daughters were standing with their hands over their heads. Edith looked distant, almost absent, Anne remained composed, and Margot cried silently.

Silberbauer wanted to know where they kept their money and other valuables. Otto pointed to the cupboard where the cash box was. Silberbauer, spying Otto's leather briefcase, turned it upside down, and shook the contents out. Anne didn't look as her diary, notebooks, and papers cascaded to the floor.

Silberbauer stuffed the now-empty briefcase with the Franks' money and jewellery and ordered a transport for his prisoners. He told everyone to return to their room and get ready to leave. They all had small bags packed in case of fire or other emergency.

Silberbauer noticed an army footlocker with Otto Frank's name and rank stencilled on it. Otto explained that he was a reserve officer in the German army during World War I. Silberbauer instinctively stiffened, nearly coming to attention. He was disturbed to find that Otto had been a German officer, and one who outranked him. Why hadn't he stepped forward before he went into hiding? They would have taken that into consideration. Given him privileged treatment.

He asked Otto how long they had been in hiding. Two years, Otto replied to a disbelieving Silberbauer. To prove it Otto took Anne and put her up against the doorjamb where they had periodically measured her height. It showed how much taller she had grown since the last time they drew a line.

Downstairs in the office, Miep Gies, shaken by that morning's events, sat helplessly in her chair, listening. She heard heavy boots on the stairs and then Anne's lighter, almost inaudible footsteps. She thought how Anne had taught herself over the two years in hiding to walk so quietly she could hardly be heard.

It was one o'clock.

Outside Kleiman, Kugler, the Franks, the van Pelses, and Pfeffer were placed in the back of a windowless police transport and driven the five minutes to Gestapo headquarters.

They were all locked in a room where other people were already waiting on the long benches. Sitting next to Kleiman, Otto apologised for involving him. Kleiman dismissed his apologies, saying he did what he had to do.

Then he and Kugler were transferred.

Silberbauer interrogated his prisoners briefly and they were returned to their cells, men separate from women.

# Westerbork

On August 8, 1944, the Franks, van Pelses, and Fritz Pfeffer were taken eighty miles north of Amsterdam to Westerbork, a sixty-acre camp created in 1939 by the Dutch government. It was a place where German Jews, fleeing their increasingly anti-Semitic homeland and hoping to find refuge in the nearby Netherlands, could be received.

In 1942, the Germans took over the camp. Inmates were now Dutch Jews, forcibly taken from their homes. There were watchtowers and a high barbed-wire fence around the perimeter. Within that was a self-sufficient city containing a large, modern kitchen, a laundry, a post office, a hospital (with 1,800 beds, 120 physicians, and a staff of 1,000), schools (all children between the ages of six and fourteen were required to attend), a tailor, a locksmith, hairdressers, a book binder and opticians. Activities included sports such as gymnastics and boxing, a choir, ballet, a camp orchestra and a cabaret show put on by the prisoners that was renowned throughout Holland for its talented performers and hard-to-get opening-night tickets. All this was calculated to keep the prison population calm and distracted, therefore minimising disturbances and resistance.

The Franks and the others were subjected to the tedious and humiliating registration process. They answered questions, filled out forms, waited in endless lines, completed more forms, and answered more questions.

> *"What I saw was a family . . . a very worried father and a nervous mother and two children . . . They had sports clothes on and backpacks with them . . . and the four of them stayed together constantly."*
>
> JANNY BRANDES-BRILLESLIJPER

> *"Mr Frank was a pleasant-looking man, courteous and cultured. He stood before me tall and erect. He answered my routine questions quietly . . . None of the Franks showed any signs of despair over their plight. Their composure, as they grouped around my typing desk in the receiving room, was one of quiet dignity. However bitter and fearful the emotions that welled in him, Mr Frank*

Because they were arrested while in hiding, all eight were assigned to the Punishment Block. Unlike other prisoners they
could not wear their own clothes. They were given blue
prison overalls with red patches (identifying them as criminals) and wooden clogs that didn't fit. They were also given
less food and more difficult work.

The day began at 5.00 a.m.

They took apart batteries with a small chisel and extracted
the manganese and carbon rods that could then be recycled to
aid the now-faltering German war machine. It was dirty,
unhealthy work that resulted in constant coughing.

Otto tried to get better work for Anne, but was unable to.

*"Otto Frank came up to me with Anne and asked if Anne
could help me. Anne was very nice and also asked me if
she could help me . . . he came to me with Anne — not
with his wife and not with Margot. I think that Anne
was the apple of his eye."*

RACHEL VAN AMERONGEN-FRANKFOORDER

Anne welcomed the chance to talk to people and be out in the fresh air after two years indoors.

"In Westerbork Anne was lovely, so radiant . . . She was very pallid at first, but there was something so intensely attractive about her frailty and her expressive face . . .

Perhaps it's not the right expression to say that Anne's eyes were radiant. But they had a glow . . . And her movements, her looks, had such a lilt to them that I often asked myself: Can she possibly be happy?"

MRS DE WIEK*

"Edith Frank, Anne's mother, seemed numbed by the experience. She could have been a mute. Anne's sister, Margot, spoke little and Otto Frank was quiet too, but his was a reassuring quietness that helped Anne and all of us. He lived in the men's barracks, but once when Anne was sick he came over to visit her every evening and would stand beside her bed for hours, telling her stories."

MRS DE WIEK

*A pseudonym

Those who were forced to exist at Westerbork did their best to keep their spirits up. They talked about the Soviet Union's Red Army advancing towards Germany; how the Germans were going to lose the war; and how it would be when it was over. Soon they could return to the life they had known. As long as they remained in Westerbork, in Holland, they would be all right.

By 1944, there were rumours — some felt more than rumours. There were concentration camps where Jewish people were being systematically murdered by Adolf Hitler's German government. Westerbork was now a "transit camp" — a "transit camp" to eastern Germany and Poland, where the concentration camps were. One hundred thousand people had been processed through the camp in the two years before the Franks' arrival. There were quotas to be filled, quotas for the trains bound for "the east". *East,* a word that once meant so little, merely a direction, was now a destination justifiably dreaded. Every Monday evening the names of those to be transferred the next morning were read out.

*"In Westerbork one lived for two days, Tuesday and Wednesday. On Thursday you start to tremble. On Fri-*

*day you were told that you were to leave on Tuesday. On Saturday you tried to get out of it. On Sunday you were told you can't get out of it. On Monday you packed . . . as much as you can. . . . On Tuesday morning, six o'clock sharp, the cattle cars left for an unknown destination . . ."*

JACK POLAK

The Nazis determined how many and when, but the Jewish administration within the camp determined who.

*"When we heard that we were on the list, we tried everything we could do to change things, but it was no good. The people who compiled the list were mainly Jews, I think, and they did what they could to protect their friends and relatives. But for the rest, well, we just had to go."*

EVA SCHLOSS

*"On 2 September we were told that a thousand persons would leave in the morning . . . During the night we packed a few things we had been allowed to keep. Someone had a little ink, and with that we marked our names on the blankets we were to take with us and we made the children repeat again and again the address where we were going to meet after the war, in case we got*

Early in the morning of September 3, 1944, the prisoners began filing out of the barracks towards the trains, which came right into the centre of the camp. The commandant, his dog, and the guards enjoyed watching what had become a weekly event.

Carrying their bundled-up belongings suspended by straps from their shoulders, as allowed, the prisoners walked in threes, as instructed.

They did not know for certain where they were going, but the rumours were terrifying.

There were 498 women, 442 men, and 79 children. Four of the men were Otto Frank, Hermann and Peter van Pels, and Fritz Pfeffer. Four of the women were Edith, Margot, and Anne Frank, and Auguste van Pels.

The train left Westerbork at 11.00 a.m. It was the ninety-third and last transport to leave Westerbork for "the east".

For Auschwitz.

All eight were in the same car. There was straw on the floor, a small bucket of water, and an empty one for elimination. There was little light and the only air came from a few holes in the roof. There was barely enough room to stand and the heat and awful smells were overwhelming.

*"When the train stopped for the first time, we were already in Germany. Some bread and a pail of beet marmalade were tossed in . . . We did not know where we were, since the train had not stopped at a station, but at a siding, and we could not ask because SS guards were patrolling up and down outside the train.*

*We stopped many times in the open country, somewhere or other, and once the train suddenly started backing, so that someone cried, 'Look! We're going back to Holland!'*

*But we did not go to Holland. We went back and forth but deeper and deeper into Germany . . . Now and then when the train stopped, the SS men came to the door and held out their caps, and we were supposed to put our money and valuables into the caps. Some of us actually had a few things left, sewed into our clothes, for instance, and there were some who took out what they had, flung it into the SS caps, and then the train went on. That was how it went, night and day, and night again."*

MRS DE WIEK

Anne watched through the cracks in the floor as the rails whizzed by and climbed up the bars so she could peer out of the small window.

*"Mrs Frank had smuggled out a pair of overalls, and she sat by the light of the candle, ripping off the red patch. She must have thought that without the red patch, they wouldn't be able to see that we were convict prisoners . . . for her it was important and she got some satisfaction from doing it.*

*Many people, among them the Frank girls, leaned against their mother or father; everyone was dead tired."*

LENIE DE JONG-VAN NAARDEN

# *Auschwitz-Birkenau*

≡ SEPTEMBER 6, 1944–OCTOBER 1944 ≡

Before March 1941, Adolf Hitler's goal had been the forced emigration of all Jews from Germany and recently conquered territories. Now that changed. The newly planned objective of the German government was the total physical annihilation of the eleven million Jewish people living in Europe.

In 1933, the German government began building a network of concentration camps. Some of these camps were for internment, some for forced labour, some in anticipation of deportation, and some, beginning in 1942, for the extermination of their inhabitants. Auschwitz-Birkenau was by far the largest and most lethal of these secretly constructed camps. The Nazis intended to keep their existence unknown to the population in the area, German citizens in general, and the world at large.

The site had been chosen because of its isolated location, which would help in that regard. In addition, there was access to rivers and rail transportation — transportation that could bring the people who were to be killed. Auschwitz's barracks, satellite camps, factories, and killing facilities eventually covered over twenty-five square miles. (For reasons of efficiency the SS — the branch of the German military responsible for implementing these plans — had turned from mass shooting to murder by poison gas.)

On the night of September 5, 1944, the transport carrying the eight from the secret annex reached its destination.

"... the train suddenly came to a stop. The doors ... were slid violently open, and the first we saw of Auschwitz were the glaring searchlights fixed on the train."

MRS DE WIEK

"We were taken, with our baggage, to a large area that was lit up by extraordinarily strong lights — so strong that I had the feeling that they were moons. I thought, We're on another planet ... and here there are three moons."

BLOEME EVERS-EMDEN

Trains were purposefully scheduled to arrive at night, adding to the feeling of confusion, helplessness, and disorientation. The night air was pierced by the fearsome sounds of barking dogs and loudspeakers crackling instructions: Anyone too weak to walk should board the nearby trucks with the red crosses painted on them. Kapos, head prisoners who helped the Nazis maintain order and discipline, hovered all around. Shaven-headed, strange-looking men in their striped uniforms whispered furtively, "Don't go into the trucks," to the uncomprehending and disbelieving new arrivals.

*"A detachment of SS men with guns, whips, and clubs in their hands attacked us, separating the men from their wives, parents from their children, the old from the young. Those who resisted . . . were beaten, kicked, and dragged away. In a few minutes we were standing in separate groups, almost unconscious with pain, fear, exhaustion, and the unbearable shock of losing our loved ones."*

DR GISELLA PERL

Otto Frank, frantically struggling to make visual contact with his family, saw only his daughter Margot and the look of terror in her eyes.

*"Now, with a handful of SS officers, the camp physician took over the direction of this infernal game. With a flick of his hand he sent some of us to the left, some to the right. It took some time before I understood what this meant. Of every trainload of prisoners, ten to twelve thousand at a time, he selected about three thousand inmates for his camp. The others, those who went 'left', were . . . carted away."*

Dr Gisella Perl

Those judged able to work as slave labour for the Third Reich were spared. Those who weren't — anyone who was sick, disabled, over fifty, under fifteen (89 per cent of the Jewish children in Europe were murdered in the death camps), pregnant, or a mother who refused to be separated from her children — were taken directly to the gas chambers.

Some were able to act transcendently:

*"I came to Auschwitz August 22, 1944. I came with my mother, my brother, my father, my aunt and uncle, and my cousin. A neighbour of ours was with us . . . He had a four-year-old child with him; he had lost his wife in the ghetto.*

*We got off the trains in Auschwitz and they separated the men right away. The women and children were on one side and the men on the other. When we got off the train and they separated the men, this little girl, the neighbour's child, was left alone. My mother (she was a saint) walked over to him and she said, 'Don't worry, I will take care of the child.' She took this child by the hand and she kept her, wouldn't let go of her. The child was alone and my mother wouldn't let the child stand alone.*

*Everything happened very rapidly ... My aunt was with her little boy in the front and my mother with this little girl by the hand and my brother, and I was the last one. My aunt and her little boy he motioned to the left, and when he asked my mother if this was her child and she nodded yes, he sent her to the left. My brother, being only twelve at the time, he sent to the left, and me he motioned to the right.*

*I realised my mother was on the other side and I wanted to run to my mother, I wanted to be with her. A Jewish woman who worked there caught me in the middle and said ... 'Don't you dare move from here!' Because she knew that if I was on the other side I would go to the gas chamber. And she wouldn't let me move ...*

*This was the last time I saw my mother. She went*

*with that neighbour's child. So when we talk about heroes, mind you, this was a hero: a woman who would not let a four-year-old child go by herself."*

ESTHER GEIZHALS-ZUCKER

Those sent "left" were told to undress and keep their clothes and shoes tied together. They were handed soap and the children were given toys. All to create the illusion that nothing bad was about to happen.

*". . . these men and women were . . . forced . . . to the 'Shower Room'. Above the entry door was the word 'Shower'. One could even see the shower heads on the ceiling which were cemented in but never had water flowing through them.*

*These poor innocents were crammed together, pressed against each other. Then panic broke out, for at last they realised the fate in store for them. But blows with rifle butts and revolver shots soon restored order and finally they all entered the death chamber.*

*One of the guards climbed up on to the roof, put his mask, gloves, and protective clothing on, and pulled a sealed tin up to him that was attached by a wire. The tin contained Zyklon-B which had previously been used to fumigate lice-infested buildings. He fed the green crystals into the duct on the roof.*

*The doors were shut and, ten minutes later, the temperature was high enough to facilitate the condensation of hydrogen cyanide . . . the so-called Zyklon-B . . . used by the German barbarians.*

*. . . One could hear the fearful screams, but a few moments later there was complete silence. Twenty to twenty-five minutes later, the doors and windows were opened to ventilate the rooms."*

ANDRÉ LETTICH

Hair, gold teeth, and wedding rings were salvaged, as well as clothes that were sent back for German citizens to wear. The soap and toys were collected for use with the next group.

One out of every ten persons arriving at Auschwitz was put to death on the first day.

In the thirty-two months that Auschwitz was in full operation as an extermination camp it is estimated that 1.1 million people, the overwhelming majority of them Jewish, were killed.

Of the 1,019 people who arrived on the September 5 transport from Westerbork, 549 were murdered immediately.

The Franks, van Pelses, and Fritz Pfeffer, sent "right", survived that first day.

Those who survived this first selection process had to watch as the smoke rose up from the chimneys of the crematoria.

> "... not far from us I could see a tall structure spewing out bright flames ... This, I thought, was one of the strangest German symbols I had ever seen. None of us had any inkling of the awful truth."
>
> ANONYMOUS AUSCHWITZ INMATE

Otto, Hermann, Peter, and Fritz Pfeffer were taken to the main slave labour camp. Edith and her two daughters and probably Mrs van Pels were taken to Birkenau, a unit of Auschwitz. All had numbers tattooed on their left forearms (something done only at Auschwitz-Birkenau).

> "... we were herded into a ... room ... smeared with disinfectant [and] ... received our prison clothing. I cannot think of any name that would fit the bizarre rags that were handed out for underwear. We asked ourselves what this 'under-clothing' was supposed to be. It was not

*white nor any other colour, but worn-out pieces of coarse*

*dusting-cloth."*

OLGA LENGYEL

Their hair was rudely cut short and they were forced to strip so they could be searched and checked for lice.

*". . . we were taken to rooms where we had to undress. That was an enormous shock for me. I was eighteen, shy, and had been brought up chastely, according to the prevailing morality. It goes without saying that I was embarrassed and ashamed. I remember an audible crack in my head, from being totally naked before the eyes of men. And then the thought came like a flash that, from then on, other norms and values would be in effect, that I would have to adjust to that, and that an entirely new life was beginning, or death was waiting."*

BLOEME EVERS-EMDEN

The secret-annexe eight, among the thousands of other new arrivals at Auschwitz-Birkenau, struggled to adjust as well as they could as quickly as they could to their new, horrific surroundings and the degrading and dehumanising daily routine.

"Each camp consisted of endless rows of blocks — dirty, rat-infested wooden barracks — housing about twelve-hundred persons each. Along the inner walls of the barracks, there were three rows of wooden shelves, one above the other, and these shelves were our bedrooms, living-rooms, dining-rooms and studies, all in one. They were divided by vertical planks at regular intervals. Each of these cage-like contraptions served as sleeping-room for thirty to thirty-six persons."

DR GISELLA PERL

"Seven or eight women had to go in each one. We called it 'lined up like spoons'. Everyone had to turn around at the same time. You couldn't lie in the positions you wanted.

The first night, a woman went outside the barracks; she was shot. That woman, horribly wounded, spent the whole night lying there, groaning. We didn't know what we should do — go out there or not — but the others shouted, 'No, no, you have to stay in bed; that's not allowed.' That woman lay there, dying, in a grue-some way. Then I knew, Yes, they really shoot people here. Early in the morning she was dead, lying in front of the barracks, and we saw that. From then on, I

167

knew for sure that they would shoot people from the towers."

Ronnie Goldstein–van Cleef

"Life in Auschwitz began at four o'clock in the morning when we had to crawl forth from our holes to stand for roll call in the narrow street separating one block from another. We stood in rows of five, at arm's length from one another, soundless and motionless for four, five, or six hours at a time, in any kind of weather, all year round . . . The number had to be complete, even the dying and the dead had to be brought out to stand at attention. If anyone did not appear, she was tracked down and thrown into the flames, alive. The same punishment was meted out to those who collapsed, fainted, or cried out with pain when hit by a whip. Often, for God knows what reason, the SS decided to punish us, and after roll call all one-hundred-and-fifty thousand of us had to kneel down in the snow or mud, to stay there on our bruised, bleeding knees for another hour or two. How often did I see women fall out of the ranks in a dead faint, without being able to succor them, to bring them even the most primitive of comforts: a glass of water."

Dr Gisella Perl

Some were so thirsty they drank water that was clearly marked poison.

After roll call, the 39,000 women, divided into work groups, marched off as the camp orchestra played. Some were assigned to squeeze toothpaste out of toothpaste tubes looking for diamonds that new arrivals might have hidden. Most worked outside, winter and summer, twelve-hour days with no rest.

Hunger was a constant, painful companion. Food consisted of an indescribable brown liquid, dry black bread that had been made partly with sawdust, thin turnip soup, and sometimes a slice of sausage or piece of cheese. There were no utensils, and if you lost your bowl you went without. Some talked about their hunger obsessively; others believed that not talking about it was the only way to survive.

There was only one latrine for the entire women's camp, resulting in endless, long lines. Most had dysentery, adding to their embarrassment and discomfort.

The ill did not seek medical treatment and tried not to show weakness. They stuffed old newspapers in their clothes so that they didn't look as malnourished as they were and tried to make their cheeks look less pale. Anything to avoid being "selected", camp jargon meaning "chosen to go to the gas chambers".

*". . . after only one week of prison, the instinct for cleanliness disappeared in me . . . Why should I wash? Would I be better off than I am? Would I please someone more? Would I live a day, an hour longer? I would probably live a shorter time, because to wash is an effort, a waste of energy and warmth."*

PRIMO LEVI

*". . . we were standing outside and I saw a wagon the first day and [said] . . . 'What's he thrown on there? Dead bodies, oh my God!' I could hardly look. The next couple of days later I saw it. [and said] 'Oh, there's that wagon again that picks up the dead bodies.' And the next time I didn't even pay any attention to that wagon. So your brain starts functioning differently, because if you don't — you didn't do it on purpose — then you couldn't go on living."*

ROSE DE LIEMA

Otto, Hermann, and Fritz Pfeffer were assigned to ditch-digging and Peter to the camp post office where the SS guards and non-Jewish prisoners received their mail. Peter's assignment enabled him to get extra rations, which he shared with his father and the other two men.

In early October 1944, Hermann van Pels injured his thumb while digging a trench and unwisely requested barracks duty. There was a "selection" among those barracks workers and Hermann van Pels was "selected" to be murdered in the gas chambers of Auschwitz. (Fritz Pfeffer had been transferred to another camp and died there on December 20, 1944.)

The average life expectancy of someone who lived past the first day of Auschwitz was between six and seven weeks. Peter and Otto were, however, holding out relatively well. Otto, true to his nature, attempted to remain positive. He shied away from anyone who complained all the time, preferring the company of those who could join him in a discussion about Beethoven and Schubert — not hunger and illness.

Edith and her two daughters stayed together, trying to help one another survive.

> *"In the period that we were in Auschwitz . . . Mrs Frank tried very hard to keep her children alive, to keep them with her, to protect them. Naturally, we spoke to each other. But you could do absolutely nothing, only give advice like, If they go to the latrine go with them. Because*

*even on the way from the barracks to the latrine, some-thing could happen."*

LENIE DE JONG–VAN NAARDEN

*"Very important [for] survival for all people in concen-tration camps were to form little groups, support groups, and of course as mother and children and daughters, you were a natural support group. And I think everything from the past was faded away against this scene of Auschwitz. It was of no importance any more I sup-pose."*

BLOEME EVERS-EMDEN

They existed without privacy, engulfed in a world of tension and terror, in constant fear of an endless list of things that could and often did bring instant death. By necessity, many became desensitised and hardened to the pervasive horror that had become daily life. Anne struggled to maintain her personality and remain human.

*"Anne seemed even more beautiful there than she had at Westerbork. Of course her long hair was gone, but now you could see that her beauty was in her eyes, which*

*seemed to grow bigger as she grew thinner. Her gaiety
had vanished, but she still was alert and sweet, and with
her charm she sometimes secured things that the rest of us
had long since given up hoping for.*

*For example, we each had only a grey sack to wear.
But when the weather turned cold, Anne came in one
day wearing a suit of men's long underwear. She had
begged it somewhere. She looked screamingly funny
with those long white legs, but somehow still delightful.*

*Though she was the youngest, Anne was the leader
in her group of five people. She also gave out the bread to
everyone in the barracks and she did it so fairly there was
none of the usual grumbling . . .*

*We scarcely saw and heard these things any longer.
Something protected us, kept us from seeing. But Anne
had no such protection, to the last. I can still see her
standing at the door and looking down the camp street as
a herd of naked gypsy girls were driven by, to the crematorium, and Anne watched them going and cried. And
she cried also when we marched past the Hungarian
children who had already been waiting half a day in the
rain in front of the gas chambers, because it was not yet
their turn. And Anne nudged me, and said: 'Look, look.
Their eyes . . .'*

*She cried. And you cannot imagine how soon most*
*of us came to the end of our tears."*

Mrs de Wiek

Their bad diets and the unsanitary conditions of the camps resulted in a variety of illnesses and disease. Anne contracted scabies, a contagious skin disease. It covered her entire body with reddish pimples and the itching, especially at night, was severe.

In late October 1944, there was a "selection". Those considered fit enough were sent to work in a munitions factory, clearly better than staying in Auschwitz. Anne, too sick, was sent to the scabies barracks, which was completely isolated from the rest of the camp.

*". . . Margot and her mother decided to stay with Anne.*
*If they could have gone with our transport they would*
*have survived because nearly everybody in my transport*
*after Auschwitz survived."*

Bloeme Evers-Emden

Margot stayed with Anne in the scabies barracks and contracted the disease there.

*"The Frank girls looked terrible, their hands and bodies covered with spots and sores from the scabies. They applied some salve, but there was not much that they could do. They were in a very bad way."*

RONNIE GOLDSTEIN–VAN CLEEF

Desperately Edith Frank searched for scraps of food for her sick daughters. A friend found a watch and gave it to Edith, who traded it for some bread, cheese, and sausages that she somehow got to her daughters.

Just days later there was yet another "selection".

*"Anne encouraged Margot, and Margot walked erect into the light. There they stood for a moment, naked and shaven-headed, and Anne looked over at us with her unclouded face, looked straight and stood straight, and they were approved and passed along. We could not see what was on the other side of the light. Mrs Frank screamed, 'The children! Oh, God!'"*

MRS DE WIEK

Anne and Margot were "selected" to be on a transport bound for Bergen-Belsen concentration camp. Their mother, having no choice, remained behind in Auschwitz.

She grew sicker and weaker by the day, dying of grief for the two daughters she could not save.

"*She was very weak and no longer eating, scarcely in her right mind. Whatever food she was given she collected under her blanket, saying that she was saving it for her husband because he needed it — and then the bread spoiled under the blanket.*

*I don't know whether she was so weakened because she was starving, or whether she had stopped eating because she was too weak to eat. There was no longer any way of telling. I watched her die without a murmur.*"

MRS DE WIEK

Edith Frank died on January 6, 1945. In ten days she would have been forty-five.

# Bergen-Belsen

$A$t the end of October 1944, the Frank sisters were on a transport headed west, back towards their birthplace, Germany.

*"When our train arrived in Belsen . . . we passed through the barbed-wire gate of the camp without really noticing it, for there was no trace of any camp. No barracks, no crematorium . . .*

*There we stood and looked around in astonishment. But soon some curious prisoners came toward us out of the wasteland. Their heads were shaved and they looked in a very bad way.*

*'Where does one live here?' I asked a woman. 'In tents,' she told me. 'We all sleep on the ground.' 'And is there water here?' 'Not much.' 'Latrines?' 'We have just*

*made a pit for ourselves.' 'And food?' 'Irregular, little of it, and bad.'*

*We knew what questions to ask when we arrived in a new camp — we had plenty of camp life . . . But there was little need to ask many questions. The indications were clear enough."*

Mrs Renate L. A. *

Established in 1941 as a prisoner-of-war camp, by 1943 Bergen-Belsen (the names of the two towns it was situated between) had become an "exchange camp". Jewish prisoners with connections abroad, the right papers, or value as hostages were sent there. Eventually they were to be exchanged for German citizens and soldiers being held by the Allies (however, very few ever were). In the meantime they would be used as slave labour for the Third Reich. Families would be allowed to stay together and would remain alive.

Since March 1944, sick and exhausted prisoners — anyone judged unable to work — had been evacuated from other concentration camps and sent to Bergen-Belsen. It was now termed a "recuperation camp" in the ironic, sadistic jar-

*A pseudonym

gon that hid its true purpose: they had been sent there to die, not recuperate.

The already overcrowded, chaotic camp was unable to properly receive the thousands of people arriving daily. The authorities at Bergen-Belsen hastily constructed tents for temporary housing.

> "... the third night I was there we had a storm. The tents ripped and flew off, and the heavy poles came crashing down on us. The next two nights we slept in a storage shed, among the heaps of SS caps and military boots. On the third day we were driven to a block of barracks that had meanwhile been cleared. That was the beginning of our stay in Belsen."
>
> Mrs Renate L. A.

The extreme overcrowding and the woeful physical condition of the new arrivals led to hunger, thirst, and rampant disease: dysentery, tuberculosis, and typhus.

There was no water for days at a time, and people died crawling towards the water pump. Some desperately boiled grass, and SS guards were needed when the vat of foul-smelling, barely edible soup was taken to the huts because someone crazed by hunger might attack it. All this occurred while hundreds of Red Cross food parcels containing Ovaltine, canned meat, milk, and biscuits remained unopened and undistributed.

"... I ran across a woman who I had known at Auschwitz. She had been a block orderly there, and had had decent clothing and food. Now here she stood holding a soup kettle, scraping it out and greedily licking the dregs. When I saw that, I knew enough. It was a bad camp where not even the privileged group had enough to eat. My sister and I looked at one another, and my sister, who had just turned sixteen, said: 'No one will come out of this camp alive.'"

Mrs Renate L. A.

"The end is the same — only the means are different. In Auschwitz it is a quick, ruthless procedure, mass murder in the gas chambers; in Belsen it is a sadistic, long drawn-out process of starvation, of violence, of terror, of the deliberate spreading of infection and disease."

Hanna Lévy-Hass

Anne and Margot clung to each other, trying to survive despite their deteriorating condition and the horror that was enveloping them.

As late fall in northern Germany turned into winter, conditions became even more severe, even more life-threatening. The freezing winds made life that much harder to endure and everyone that much sicker.

Anne and Margot saw a woman they had met at Auschwitz:

*"Anne used to tell stories after we lay down. So did Margot. Silly stories and jokes. We all took our turns telling them. Mostly they were about food. Once we talked about going to the American Hotel in Amsterdam for dinner and Anne suddenly burst into tears at the thought that we would never get back . . . we compiled a menu, masses of wonderful things to eat."*

LIENTJE BRILLESLIJPER-JALDATI

*"The Frank girls were almost unrecognisable since their hair had been cut off. They were much balder than we were; how that could be, I don't know. And they were cold, just like the rest of us.*

*It was winter and you didn't have any clothes. So all of the ingredients for illness were present. They were in bad shape. Day by day they got weaker. Nevertheless they went to the fence of the so-called free camp every day, in the hopes of getting something. They were very determined. I'm virtually certain that they met someone there whom they knew."*

RACHEL VAN AMERONGEN–FRANKFOORDER

By the spring of 1944, the overwhelming majority of those living in the so-called Free Camp, a subcamp within Bergen-Belsen, were Dutch. Among them was Lies Goslar, Anne's good friend from Amsterdam.

Lies Goslar's mother had died, along with the baby, giving birth after the Franks went into hiding. In June 1943, Lies, her father, and little sister, Gabi, were rounded up by the Nazis. Because their names were on a list to immigrate to Palestine they were sent from Westerbork to the Free Camp at Bergen-Belsen in February 1944, six months before Anne and the others were discovered in hiding.

In early February 1945, Lies heard that Dutch women from Auschwitz were in the adjacent camp.

*"One day a friend of mine tells me, 'You know, between all these women there is your friend Anne Frank.' And I don't know I felt very crazy because I was thinking the whole time Anne is safe and she's in Switzerland. I was sure of this, but this was what [she] said to me and so I had no choice but to go . . . near this barbed wire — this was not allowed. And the German in the watchtower was watching us and you know he would have shot if he would have caught us, but — so we couldn't see . . . there was a barbed wire with straw and we couldn't see the other side. So, I just went near at dark and I would start to call hello, hello? something like this and who answered me but Mrs van Pels . . . She said 'You want Anna . . . I will call her for you. Margot I can't call for you, she is very sick already, but Anna I will call for you.'"*

HANNELI ELISABETH "LIES" PICK-GOSLAR

Auguste van Pels told Lies that Margot was too sick to come but she would get Anne. Separated by the barbed wire the two friends cried; then Anne spoke:

*"She said, 'We don't have anything at all to eat here, almost nothing, and we are cold; we don't have any*

clothes and I've gotten very thin and they shaved my hair.' That was terrible for her. She had always been very proud of her hair. It may have grown back a bit in the meantime, but it certainly wasn't the long hair she'd had before, which she playfully curled around her fingers . . .

We agreed to meet the next evening at eight o'-clock . . . I succeeded in throwing [a] package [of food] over.

But I heard her screaming, and I called out, 'What happened?'

And Anne answered, 'Oh, the woman standing next to me caught it, and she won't give it back to me.'

Then she began to scream.

I calmed her down a bit and said, 'I'll try again but I don't know if I'll be able to.' We arranged to meet again, two or three days later, and I was actually able to throw over another package. She caught it: that was the main thing.

After these three or four meetings at the barbed-wire fence in Bergen-Belsen, I didn't see her again, because the people in Anne's camp were transferred to another section of Bergen-Belsen. That happened around the end

*of February. That was the last time I saw Anne alive and*
*spoke to her."*

HANNELI ELISABETH "LIES" PICK-GOSLAR

Anne was horrified by the lice and had thrown all of her clothes away, even though it was the middle of the winter. She just walked around with a blanket wrapped around her. Both girls had typhus and looked emaciated.

*"They were terribly cold. They had the least desirable place in the barracks, below, near the door, which was constantly opened and closed. You heard them constantly screaming, 'Close the door, close the door,' and their voices became weaker every day.*

*You could really see both of them dying ... They were ... the youngest among us."*

RACHEL VAN AMERONGEN–FRANKFOORDER

*"It had to have been in March, as the snow was already melting as we went to look for them, but they weren't in the bunk any longer. In the quarantine (sick bunk) is where we found them. We begged them not to stay there, as people in there deteriorated so quickly and couldn't*

185

*bring themselves to resist, that they'd be soon at the end. Anne simply said, 'Here we both can lie on the plank bed; we'll be together and at peace.' Margot only whispered; she had a high fever.*

*The following day we went to them again. Margot had fallen from the bed, just barely conscious. Anne also was feverish, yet she was friendly and sweet. 'Margot's going to sleep well, and when she sleeps, I won't have to stay up.'"*

LIENTJE BRILLESLIJPER-JALDATI

*"Anne was sick, too, but she stayed on her feet until Margot died; only then did she give in to her illness."*

JANNY BRANDES-BRILLESLIJPER

Anne, after watching her older sister slowly die, on or near her nineteenth birthday, lost her will to live.

Days later, sometime in late February or early March 1945, Annelies Marie Frank, fifteen, perished, her body thrown in a mass grave.

One month later, on April 15, 1945, Bergen-Belsen was liberated by British soldiers.

# PART FOUR

# SURVIVING

$B$y the fall of 1944, Hitler's regime, knowing they were going to lose the war, began destroying the physical and documentary evidence of their monstrous crimes.

They ordered the destruction of the Auschwitz-Birkenau killing machine: dynamiting the crematoria, demolishing the electrified barbed-wire fence and guard towers, and burning incriminating documents. They packed up piles of the remaining clothing, eyeglasses, and suitcases belonging to the 1.1 million people whose lives they had taken at Auschwitz, and sent them back to Berlin for use by German civilians. Left behind in the rush were 348,820 suits for men and 836,516 dresses. They dug up the dead bodies that had been thrown into the mass graves and burned them in open pits. And they ordered an end to the gassings. There were no more at

Auschwitz after November 1944, although random killings continued.

On January 16, 1945, ten days after Edith Frank died and only a few weeks before her daughters did, Russian planes began attacking Auschwitz. Soon inmates could hear artillery and automatic-weapon fire.

Leaving the seven thousand sick and injured behind, the Germans began to flee, fearing the advancing Russian army.

Anyone who could walk was forced to march out with them. Those sixty thousand inmates were to be taken and dispersed to other concentration camps, presumably located further away from the fast-approaching Allied forces.

In the snow and bitter cold, wearing little to protect them and already half dead from months and years of deprivation, they moved out on what was to become a death march. Thousands died from disease, illness, hunger, thirst, and exhaustion, and thousands more, unable to keep up, were shot and left by the side of the road.

One percent of all those sent to Auschwitz survived.

One of them was Otto Frank.


Two months earlier, in November 1944, weak and ill from the slave labour and beatings, Otto was losing hope.

*"One day in Auschwitz I was very depressed, I had been
beaten the day before and that really affected me ... It was
a Sunday morning and I said, 'I can't get up' and then my
comrades ... said to me, 'That's not possible ... you must
get up otherwise you are lost.' And then they went to a
Dutch doctor who worked with a German doctor and this
Dutch doctor came to me in my barracks. He said, 'Get up
and come tomorrow morning to the sick barracks and I'll
speak to the German doctor so that you will be accepted.'
And that is what happened and through that I was saved."*

Peter van Pels dutifully visited Otto in the hospital. Otto
tried to persuade Peter to stay with him and hide in the
hospital. But fearing that he might be shot if found and
believing he was in good enough physical condition to with-
stand the rigors of the evacuation march, Peter left.

Peter van Pels was right — he was in good enough shape
to survive the march. However, on May 5, 1945, he died
in the Mauthausen concentration camp, just days before
American soldiers liberated it.

Auguste van Pels had been transferred from Bergen-
Belsen to an unknown destination. It is believed she died in
the spring of 1945.

Otto Frank and the other survivors still at Auschwitz summoned the strength to wave and shake the hands of their liberators. They were given food to eat, and doctors and nurses came to tend to them. However, many were too ill and their liberators had come too late. Thousands died in the days and weeks that followed.

Otto Frank was free, but like so many others he had no job, no money, no home to return to, and no future. He knew nothing of the fate of his family.

In May 1945, he wrote to his mother:

*Dearest Mother . . . All my hope is the children. I cling to the conviction that they are alive and that we will be together again. Unfortunately Edith did not survive. She died on January 6, 1945, in the hospital of starvation . . . What happened in all these years, we own nothing any more. We won't find a pin when we get back. The Germans stole everything: no photograph, no letter, no documents will remain there. Financially, we had no worries during the last years. I earned good money and saved. Now all is gone. But I don't worry about this — we have gone through too much to worry about things like that. Only the children, the children are what count.*

On June 3, 1945, Otto Frank returned to Amsterdam.

Living with Miep Gies and her husband, he returned to work at his old company and spent the rest of his time searching in chaotic postwar Holland for news of his children. He contacted groups of survivors as they returned, asking if anyone knew of his two daughters. He placed ads in the "Information Requested About" section of the newspaper:

MARGOT FRANK (19) AND ANNA FRANK (16) IN JAN. ON TRANS. FROM BERGEN-BELSEN. O. FRANK, PRINSENGRACHT 263, TEL. 37059.

Those who were returning to Holland from the concentration camps were asked to put crosses next to the names of anyone whose fate they were aware of on the long lists that were posted.

Two sisters who had known the Frank girls in Auschwitz and then at the end in Bergen-Belsen did that, and Otto was notified. After having this information confirmed in person, Otto Frank now knew that his family was no more.

On the day the Franks, the van Pelses, and Fritz Pfeffer were discovered in hiding, Miep Gies returned to the secret annexe that afternoon.

Everything was a mess as the Germans, looking for anything of value, had torn the rooms apart. Still scattered on the floor where they had been dumped from Otto's briefcase were Anne's diary, notebooks, and tissue-thin coloured papers that she wrote on.

Knowing that the Germans would soon be coming back with a moving van to pack up all the furniture and everything else and ship it back to Germany, Miep gathered up all the papers and put the diary in her desk.

She had never read the diary, considering it private and hoping to return it to Anne after the war.

Now, hearing that Anne was not coming home:

*"I took out all the papers, placing the little red-orange checkered diary on top, and carried everything into Mr Frank's office.*

*Frank was sitting at his desk, his eyes murky with shock. I held out the diary and the papers to him. I said, 'Here is your daughter Anne's legacy to you.'*

*I could tell that he recognised the diary. He had given it to her just over three years before, on her thirteenth birthday, right before going into hiding. He touched it with the tips of his fingers. I pressed everything into his hands; then I left his office, closing the door quietly."*

Otto wanted friends and relatives to read Anne's diary. After taking out some entries that he considered offensive (Anne's writing about her bodily development and her tumultuous relationship with her mother), he typed up copies to be read. Those who read it felt it should be published. Dutch publishers, believing that people were not interested in reading anything about the recently ended war, were themselves not interested.

One of the people who read the diary and believed it deserved a wider audience was Dr Jan Romein, a well-known Dutch historian. In April 1946, he published in the newspaper an article called "A Child's Voice". The article kindled interest in the diary, which was published in 1947 in Dutch. French, English, and American editions followed. The American edition was published in 1952 after being rejected by ten publishers.

Nearly twenty-five million copies in sixty different languages of Annelies Marie Frank's diary have been sold worldwide.

*I shall not remain insignificant.*

— ANNE FRANK

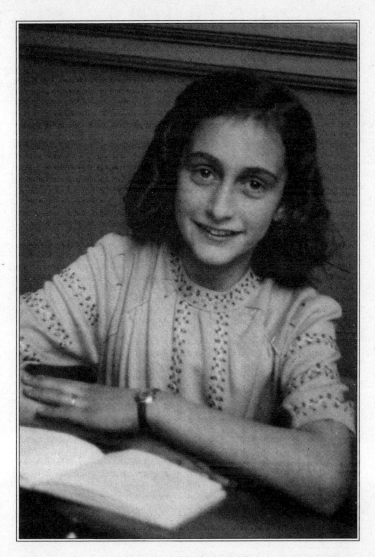

*Anne Frank (1929-1945)*

# CHRONOLOGY

**MAY 12, 1889:** Otto Frank born Frankfurt, Germany

**JANUARY 16, 1900:** Edith Holländer born Aachen, Germany

**1914–1918:** World War I

**MAY 12, 1925:** Otto Frank and Edith Holländer marry

**1925:** *Mein Kampf* (*My Struggle*), autobiography of Adolf Hitler, published

**FEBRUARY 16, 1926:** Margot Betti Frank born Frankfurt, Germany

**JUNE 12, 1929:** Annelies Marie Frank born Frankfurt, Germany

**OCTOBER 28, 1929:** New York Stock Exchange crashes; worldwide economic crisis follows

**1933:**

- Adolf Hitler appointed German chancellor
- Nazis begin passing anti-Jewish laws
- First concentration camps established

**DECEMBER 1933–FEBRUARY 1934:** The Franks move to Amsterdam, Holland

**MARCH 12, 1938:** German army invades and annexes Austria

**SEPTEMBER 29, 1938:** Munich Treaty — England and France allow Germany to occupy neighbouring territory

NOVEMBER 9–10, 1938: *Kristallnacht*, "Night of the Broken Glass"; anti-Jewish rioting occurs throughout Germany

1939: Westerbork refugee camp created by Dutch government

AUGUST 23, 1939: Germany and the Soviet Union sign a non-aggression pact

SEPTEMBER 1, 1939: Germany attacks Poland, forcing England and France to declare war on Germany

1939–1940: Deportation of European Jews into ghettos and concentration camps begins

1940: Auschwitz concentration camp established

≡ Germany attacks and defeats Denmark, Norway, Belgium, Luxembourg, Holland, and France

MAY 10, 1940: Germany invades Belgium, Luxembourg, France, and Holland; five days later the Dutch occupation begins

≡ Anti-Jewish laws instituted in Holland over following two years

1941: Bergen-Belsen prisoner-of-war camps established

JUNE 1941: Germany invades the Soviet Union

DECEMBER 7, 1941: Japan attacks the U.S. military base at Pearl Harbor, Hawaii, bringing America into the war

1942: Westerbork transformed by Germans into a labour camp

JANUARY 20, 1942: Wannsee (Berlin suburb) Conference — high-ranking Nazi officials devise plans for the extermination of all Jews in Europe

**May 1942:** The first mass gassings at Auschwitz occur

**June 12, 1942:** Anne Frank receives a diary for her thirteenth birthday

**July 5, 1942:** The Franks receive a notice ordering Margot to report for deportation to Westerbork

**July 6, 1942:** The Frank family goes into hiding in the annexe behind Otto Frank's office

**July 13, 1942:** The van Pels family joins the Frank family in hiding

**November 16, 1942:** Friedrich "Fritz" Pfeffer joins the two families in hiding

**1943:** Bergen-Belsen becomes an "exchange camp"

**February 2, 1943:** The German army surrenders to the Russians at Stalingrad

**September 8, 1943:** Italy surrenders to the Allies

**1944:** Bergen-Belsen becomes a "recuperation camp"

**June 6, 1944:** D-day — the long-awaited Allied invasion of Europe at Normandy, France, begins

**July 20, 1944:** German army officers fail in assassination attempt on Hitler's life

**August 4, 1944:** Those hiding in the annexe are betrayed, discovered, and arrested

**August 8, 1944:** All eight are taken to Westerbork

**September 3, 1944:** All eight are taken to Auschwitz-Birkenau concentration camp in Poland

**OCTOBER 1944:** Hermann van Pels dies

**LATE OCTOBER 1944:** Anne and Margot are taken to Bergen-Belsen concentration camp

**DECEMBER 20, 1944:** Fritz Pfeffer dies in Neuengamme concentration camp

**JANUARY 6, 1945:** Edith Frank dies in Auschwitz-Birkenau

**JANUARY 27, 1945:** Auschwitz is liberated by the Soviet Union's Red Army; survivors include Otto Frank

**LATE FEBRUARY–EARLY MARCH 1945:** Anne and Margot Frank die of typhus in Bergen-Belsen concentration camp

**SPRING 1945:** Auguste van Pels dies

**APRIL 15, 1945:** Bergen-Belsen is liberated by British soldiers

**MAY 5, 1945:** Peter van Pels dies in Mauthausen concentration camp
   ≡ Holland is liberated

**MAY 8, 1945:** Germany surrenders unconditionally to the Allies

**JUNE 3, 1945:** Otto Frank returns to Amsterdam

**SUMMER 1945:** Otto Frank learns that Anne and Margot have died in Bergen-Belsen; is given his daughter Anne's diary by Miep Gies

**AUGUST 6 AND 9, 1945:** The United States drops atomic bombs on the Japanese cities of Hiroshima and Nagasaki

**AUGUST 14, 1945:** Japan surrenders

**1946:** "A Child's Voice" is published

**1947:** First [Dutch] edition of Anne Frank's diary is published

**1952:** *The Diary of a Young Girl* is published in the United States

**1955:** The play *The Diary of Anne Frank* opens on Broadway; wins a Pulitzer Prize and Tony Award

**1959:** The film *The Diary of Anne Frank* is released in the United States; wins three Academy Awards

**1980:** Otto Frank dies

# A BIBLIOGRAPHICAL ESSAY

## ≡ GENERAL ≡

*Roses from the Earth: The Biography of Anne Frank*, by Carol Ann Lee, and Melissa Müller's *Anne Frank: The Biography* are two thoroughly researched and well-written recent biographies.

Ernst Schnabel's *The Footsteps of Anne Frank* (published in the United States as *Anne Frank: A Portrait in Courage*) was one of the first books (1958), if not *the* first book, written about her. Schnabel interviewed forty-two people who knew Anne; it is these interviews that many subsequent books, including mine, are based on.

Schnabel uses pseudonyms for some of the interviewees who, presumably, did not want their real names used. Anne, fearful and protective in hiding, used pseudonyms for all the people mentioned in her diary. We can see from Schnabel's book that even thirteen years after the war had ended the fear remained.

I read all three numerous times and referred to them frequently while writing *Shadow Life*.

203

Amos Elon's *The Pity of It All: A History of the Jews in Germany, 1743–1933* helped me appreciate the fullness of everyday life that was the good fortune of many Jewish families. A fullness that explains their reluctance to leave their homes and their homeland in the years following 1933 and the coming to power of Adolf Hitler.

Richard J. Evans's *The Coming of the Third Reich* and Ian Kershaw's two-volume biography of Adolf Hitler, both perceptive and scholarly works, provided a political context for those same years.

To add colour and texture to my portrait of Anne and her family a number of books were helpful. Ruud van der Rol and Rian Verhoeven's *Anne Frank: Beyond the Diary — A Photographic Remembrance* is meticulously annotated, adding to its visual qualities. Susan Goldman Rubin's *Searching for Anne Frank: Letters from Amsterdam to Iowa* is the story of Anne and Margot's pen-pal relationship with two sisters from Danville, Iowa. It is an important recent contribution to the literature on Anne Frank and allows us to read Anne and Margot's actual letters.

Two of Anne's best friends, Hanneli "Lies" Goslar (*Memories of Anne Frank: Reflections of a Childhood Friend*) and Jacqueline van Maarsen (*My Friend Anne Frank*), have published personal accounts that are anecdotal, honest, and illuminating.

Marion A. Kaplan's *Between Dignity and Despair: Jewish Life in Nazi Germany* and Deborah Dwork's *Children With a Star: Jewish Youth in Nazi Europe* educated me about the effects the rise of fascism and the increase in anti-Semitism had on everyday life. Andy Marino's *Herschel: The Boy Who Started World War II* answered questions I have had for years.

For specific background on the Jewish community in the Netherlands, the occupation, and the subsequent fate of that community, Dr J. Presser's exhaustive and definitive *Ashes in the Wind: The Destruction of Dutch Jewry* was invaluable. It allowed me to convey, via Margot's diary, some insight into the activities of the Dutch underground during the war.

## ≡PART TWO: HIDING≡

Anne's diary was, of course, my main source for information on the family's two years in hiding. It is available in a number of editions: The one I used was *The Diary of Anne Frank: The Revised Critical Edition*. This edition allowed me to read what is essentially three versions of the diary: the one Anne originally wrote from the time she was first given her diary as a birthday present; the additions and revisions she made as she prepared it for potential publication; and the diary as it was eventually edited, translated, and published. The A, B, C serial layout takes some time getting used to but it is worth the effort.

*The Revised Critical Edition* contains a number of essays that were helpful in other areas as well: the early years of the Frank family; their time in Frankfurt and Amsterdam; the establishment of Otto's business; the decision and preparations to go into hiding; the betrayal and the subsequent fate of all.

Miep Gies is a transcendent person. Her book *Anne Frank Remembered* provides a unique look at the Frank family and the events that eventually overwhelmed them.

For background on Margot's interest in Zionism and her dreams of immigrating to what was to become Israel, Walter Laqueur's *A History of Zionism* is complete and compelling.

## ≡PART THREE: DYING≡

To reconstruct the months following the arrest of the Frank family, Schnabel's book and Willy Lindwer's *The Last Seven Months of Anne Frank* were my constant reliable guides.

Over the years I have read numerous books on Nazi Germany and the Holocaust. Conceptual research for writing Part Three of this book was based on Daniel Jonah

Goldhagen's *Hitler's Willing Executioners: Ordinary Germans and the Holocaust* and Christopher R. Browning's *The Origins of the Final Solution: The Evolution of Nazi Jewish Policy, September 1939–March 1942* as well as the Evans and Kershaw books already mentioned.

Presser's book, along with Schnabel's and Lindwer's, were my main sources for information on Westerbork. To try to understand the conception, construction, and operation of Auschwitz, I referred to Yisrael Gutman and Michael Berenbaum's *Anatomy of the Auschwitz Death Camp*, Deborah Dwork and Robert Jan van Pelt's *Auschwitz: 1270 to the Present*, and Danuta Czech's *Auschwitz Chronicle: 1939–1945*, which is a harrowing day-by-day account of how death came to the inmates trapped there.

I read many first-person accounts, which shaped Part Three. Five were particularly poetic and moving: Olga Lengyel's *Five Chimneys,* Gisella Perl's *I Was a Doctor in Auschwitz,* Sara Nomberg-Przytyk's *True Tales from a Grotesque Land,* Elie Wiesel's *The Night Trilogy,* and Rudolf Vrba's *I Cannot Forgive.* Vrba managed to escape from Auschwitz and bring the first eyewitness documentation of the operations there to the outside world.

A true understanding of the Holocaust eluded me, however. As Elie Wiesel so eloquently puts it:

*"We shall never understand. Even if we manage somehow to learn every aspect of that insane project, we will never understand it . . . I think I must have read all the books— memoirs, documents, scholarly essays and testimonies written on the subject. I understand it less and less."*

## ≡ VIDEOS ≡

The above are all books, but two videos were essential to the writing of *Shadow Life*. Jon Blair's Academy Award–winning documentary *Anne Frank Remembered* played a key role in motivating me to write a book on Anne Frank for young readers, and its influence is throughout my book. The film *Anne Frank* is artfully directed, carefully cast, and beautifully acted. It is based on Müller's book and presents a dramatic and driving narrative without sacrificing historical accuracy. Both films are superlative, each in its own way.

## ≡ "WHO OWNS ANNE FRANK?" ≡

Cynthia Ozick's 1997 *New Yorker* article "Who Owns Anne Frank?" was, as I said in the Introduction, the inspiration for *Shadow Life*. The history of the diary and its publication, the agonising story of the production and staging of the 1955 play, and the way the diary has been presented and perceived over the past half century is a complicated and complex story in itself. Reading either of the two excellent books on this, Ralph Melnick's *The Stolen Legacy of Anne Frank* or Lawrence Graver's *An Obsession with Anne Frank*, will provide fertile ground for further thought.

Watching the 1959 movie, which is now available on DVD, is instructive and disturbing because of its romanticized point of view. (Seeing the original movie poster is, alone, an unsettling experience.)

A complete bibliography follows. Readers wishing to contact me with questions can write to me c/o Hodder Children's Books, 338 Euston Road, London NW1 3BH.

# BIBLIOGRAPHY

## BOOKS

ANNE FRANK STICHTING. *Anne Frank in the World, 1929–1945*. Amsterdam: Uitgeverij Bert Bakker, 1985.

BARNOUW, DAVID, AND GERROLD VAN DER STROOM, EDS. *The Diary of Anne Frank: The Critical Edition*. New York: Doubleday, 1986. *The Diary of Anne Frank: The Revised Critical Edition*. New York: Doubleday, 2001.

BLACK, EDWIN. *IBM and the Holocaust: The Strategic Alliance Between Nazi Germany and America's Most Powerful Corporation*. New York: Crown, 2001.

BLOOM, HAROLD, ED. *A Scholarly Look at the Diary of Anne Frank*. Philadelphia: Chelsea House, 1999.

BREITMAN, RICHARD. *Official Secrets: What the Nazis Planned, What the British and Americans Knew*. New York: Hill and Wang, 1998.

BRENDON, PIERS. *The Dark Valley: A Panorama of the 1930s*. New York: Alfred A. Knopf, 2000.

BROWNING, CHRISTOPHER R. *The Origins of the Final Solution: The Evolution of Nazi Jewish Policy, September 1939–March 1942*. Lincoln: University of Nebraska Press, 2004.

CARROLL, JAMES. *Constantine's Sword: The Church and the Jews*. Boston: Houghton-Mifflin, 2001.

CZECH, DANUTA. *Auschwitz Chronicle: 1939–1945*. New York: Henry Holt, 1989.

DAWIDOWICZ, LUCY S. *The War Against the Jews: 1933–1945*. New York: Holt, Rinehart and Winston, 1975.

DeCosta, Denise. *Anne Frank and Etty Hillesum: Inscribing Spirituality and Sexuality.* New Brunswick, N.J.: Rutgers University Press, 1988.

Dickens, Charles. *A Tale of Two Cities.* New York: The Modern Library, 1996.

Dwork, Deborah. *Children with a Star: Jewish Youth in Nazi Europe.* New Haven, Conn.: Yale University Press, 1991.

Dwork, Deborah, and Robert Jan van Pelt. *Auschwitz: 1270 to the Present.* New York: W.W. Norton and Company, 1996.

Elon, Amos. *Founder: A Portrait of the First Rothschild and His Time.* New York: Viking, 1996. *The Pity of It All: A History of the Jews in Germany, 1743–1933.* New York: Metropolitan Books, 2002.

Enzer, Hyman A., and Sandra Solotaroff-Enzer, eds. *Anne Frank: Reflections on Her Life and Legacy.* Urbana: University of Illinois Press, 2000.

Evans, Richard J. *The Coming of the Third Reich.* New York: The Penguin Press, 2004.

Frank, Anne. *The Diary of a Young Girl.* New York: Bantam Books, 1993.

Frank, Otto. *The Diary of a Young Girl: The Definitive Edition.* New York: Doubleday, 1991.

Friedrich, Otto. *The Kingdom of Auschwitz.* New York: Harper Perennial, 1986.

Gies, Miep, with Alison Leslie Gold. *Anne Frank Remembered: The Story of the Woman Who Helped Hide the Frank Family.* New York: Touchstone, 1987.

Goethe, Johann Wolfgang von. *The Sorrows of Young Werther* and *Novella.* New York: Vintage Classics, 1990.

Gold, Alison Leslie. *Memories of Anne Frank: Reflections of a Childhood Friend.* New York: Scholastic Inc., 1997.

GOLDHAGEN, DANIEL JONAH. *Hitler's Willing Executioners: Ordinary Germans and the Holocaust.* New York: Alfred A. Knopf, 1996. *A Moral Reckoning: The Role of the Catholic Church in the Holocaust and Its Unfulfilled Duty of Repair.* New York: Alfred A. Knopf, 2002.

GRAVER, LAWRENCE. *An Obsession with Anne Frank: Meyer Levin and the Diary.* Berkeley: University of California Press, 1995.

GRUN, BERNHARD. *The Timetables of History: A Horizontal Linkage of People and Events.* New York: Touchstone, 1963.

GUTMAN, YISRAEL, AND MICHAEL BERENBAUM. *Anatomy of the Auschwitz Death Camp.* Bloomington: Indiana University Press, 1998.

HEINE, HEINRICH. *Songs of Love and Grief.* Evanston, Ill.: Northwestern University Press, 1995.

HELLMAN, PETER, TEXT. *The Auschwitz Album: A Book Based Upon an Album Discovered by a Concentration Camp Survivor, Lili Meier.* New York: Random House, 1981.

HILBERG, RAUL. *The Destruction of the European Jews: Revised and Definitive Edition.* New York: Holmes and Meier, 1985.

HILLESUM, ETTY. *An Interrupted Life & Letters from Westerbork.* New York: Henry Holt and Co., 1996.

JOHNSON, ERIC A. *Nazi Terror: The Gestapo, Jews, and Ordinary Germans.* New York: Basic Books, 1999.

JONG, LOUIS DE. *The Netherlands and Nazi Germany.* Cambridge, Mass.: Harvard University Press, 1990.

KAPLAN, MARION A. *Between Dignity and Despair: Jewish Life in Nazi Germany.* New York: Oxford University Press, 1998.

KERSHAW, IAN. *Hitler 1889–1936 Hubris.* New York: W.W. Norton, 1998. *Hitler 1936–1945 Nemesis.* New York: W.W. Norton, 2000.

KLEMPERER, VICTOR. *I Will Bear Witness: A Diary of the Nazi Years 1933–1941*. New York: Random House, 1998. *I Will Bear Witness: A Diary of the Nazi Years 1942–1945*. New York: Random House, 1999.

KOLB, EBERHARD. *Bergen-Belsen: From 1943 to 1945*. Göttingen, Germany: Vandernhoek & Ruprecht, 1998.

KOPF, HEDDA ROSNER. *Understanding Anne Frank's Diary of a Young Girl*. Westport, Conn.: Greenwood Press, 1997.

LAQUEUR, WALTER. A *History of Zionism: From the French Revolution to the Establishment of the State of Israel*. New York: Schocken Books, 2003.

LEE, CAROL ANN. *The Hidden Life of Otto Frank*. New York: William Morrow, 2002. *Roses from the Earth: The Biography of Anne Frank*. New York: Viking, 1999.

LEITNER, ISABELLA, AND IRVING A. LEITNER. *Isabella: From Auschwitz to Freedom*. New York: Anchor Books, 1994.

LENGYEL, OLGA. *Five Chimneys: A Woman Survivor's True Story of Auschwitz*. Chicago: Academy Chicago Publishers, 1995.

LEVI, PRIMO. *Survival in Auschwitz*. New York: Touchstone, 1996.

LÉVY-HASS, HANNA. *Inside Belsen*. Sussex, England: The Harvester Press, 1982.

LINDWER, WILLY. *The Last Seven Months of Anne Frank*. New York: Anchor Books, 1991.

MAARSEN, JACQUELINE VAN. *My Friend Anne Frank*. New York: Vantage Press, 1996.

MARINO, ANDY. *Herschel: The Boy Who Started World War II*. Boston: Faber and Faber, 1995.

MELNICK, RALPH. *The Stolen Legacy of Anne Frank: Meyer Levin, Lillian Hellman and the Staging of the Diary*. New Haven, Conn.: Yale University Press, 1997.

MERTI, BETTY. *The World of Anne Frank: Readings, Activities and Resources*. Portland, Maine: J. Weston Walch, 1984.

METZGER, LOIS. *Yours, Anne: The Life of Anne Frank*. New York: Scholastic Inc., 2004.

MOORE, BOB. *Victims and Survivors: The Nazi Persecution of the Jews in the Netherlands, 1940–1945*. London: Arnold, 1997.

MÜLLER, MELISSA. *Anne Frank: The Biography*. New York: Metropolitan Books, 1998.

NOMBERG-PRZYTYK, SARA. *True Tales from a Grotesque Land*. Chapel Hill: The University of North Carolina Press, 1985.

PERL, GISELLA. *I Was a Doctor in Auschwitz*. North Stratford, N.H.: Ayer Company, 1997.

PRESSER, DR. J. *Ashes in the Wind: The Destruction of Dutch Jewry*. Detroit, Mich.: Wayne State University Press, 1988.

PRESSER, MIRJAM. *Anne Frank: A Hidden Life*. New York: Puffin Books, 2001.

READ, ANTHONY, AND DAVID FISHER. *Kristallnacht: The Nazi Night of Terror*. New York: Random House, 1989.

REILLY, JO, AND DAVID CESARANI, TONY KUSHNER, AND COLIN RICHMOND, EDS. *Belsen in History and Memory*. London: Frank Cass, 1997.

ROL, RUUD VAN DER, AND RIAN VERHOEVEN. *Anne Frank: Beyond the Diary — A Photographic Remembrance*. New York: Viking, 1993.

RUBIN, SUSAN GOLDMAN. *Searching for Anne Frank: Letters from Amsterdam to Iowa*. New York: Harry N. Abrams, 2003.

Sammons, Jeffrey L. *Heinrich Heine: A Modern Biography*. Princeton, N.J.: Princeton University Press, 1979.

Schnabel, Ernst. *The Footsteps of Anne Frank*. London: Pan Books, 1958.

Shirer, William L. *The Rise and Fall of the Third Reich: A History of Nazi Germany*. New York: Simon and Schuster, 1960.

Spiegelman, Art. *Maus I: A Survivor's Tale — My Father Bleeds History*. New York: Pantheon, 1986.

Spielberg, Steven, and Survivors of the Shoah Visual History Foundation. *The Last Days*. New York: St. Martin's, 1999.

Steenmeijer, Anna G. *A Tribute to Anne Frank*. Garden City, N.Y.: Doubleday, 1971.

Stroom, Gerrold van der, and Susan Massotty. *Anne Frank's Tales from the Secret Annex*. New York: Bantam Books, 2003.

Vrba, Rudolf, with Alan Bestic. *I Cannot Forgive*. Vancouver, B.C.: Regent College Publishing, 1964.

Wetterau, Bruce. *The New York Public Library Book of Chronologies*. New York: Prentice Hall Press, 1990.

Wiesel, Elie. *The Night Trilogy*. New York: Hill and Wang, 1985.

Wyman, David S. *The Abandonment of the Jews: America and the Holocaust, 1941–1945*. New York: Pantheon, 1984.


## ARTICLES

Buruma, Ian. "The Afterlife of Anne Frank." *The New York Review of Books*, February 19, 1998.

Melnick, Ralph, Reply by Ian Buruma. "Anne Frank's Afterlife, Cont'd." A letter. *The New York Review of Books*, May 28, 1998.

OZICK, CYNTHIA, Reply by Ian Buruma. "Anne Frank's Afterlife." A letter. *The New York Review of Books*, April 9, 1998.

OZICK, CYNTHIA. "Who Owns Anne Frank?" *The New Yorker*, October 6, 1997.

## VIDEOGRAPHY

*Amen*. A film by Costa-Gavras. Katharina/Renn Productions, 2002.

*The American Experience: America and the Holocaust: Deceit and Indifference*. WGBH Educational Foundation, 1994.

*Anne Frank*. Buena Vista Home Entertainment, 2001.

*Anne Frank Remembered*. Sony Pictures/The Jon Blair Film Company, 1995.

*Anne Frank: The Life of a Young Girl*. A&E Biography, 1999.

*The Attic: The Hiding of Anne Frank*. Cabin Fever Entertainment, 1992.

*The Diary of Anne Frank*. Twentieth Century Fox, 1959.

*The Grey Zone*. A Film by Tim Blake Nelson. Lions Gate Home Entertainment, 2002.

*The Last Seven Months of Anne Frank*. The Willy Lindwer Collection. 1988 Ergo Media Inc., 1995.

*Leni Riefenstahl's Triumph of the Will*. Synapse Films, 2001.

*Steven Spielberg and the Shoah Foundation Present: The Last Days: A Film by James Moll*. USA Home Entertainment. October Films, 1999.

# RECOMMENDED READING

ANNE FRANK HOUSE, (2001), *The World of Anne Frank,* London: Macmillan.

DAVIDOWITZ, LUCY S, (1987), *The War Against the Jews,* London: Penguin.

*The Diary of Anne Frank,* Critical Edition, (1989), New York and London: Doubleday/Viking.

FRANK, OTTO H. AND PRESSLER, MIRIAM, TRANSLATED BY SUSAN MASSOTTY, (1995), *Anne Frank: The Diary of a Young Girl,* New York: Doubleday; (1997), London: Penguin.

GIES, MIEP WITH GOLD, ALISON LESLIE, (1988), *Anne Frank Remembered,* Simon & Schuster Inc.

GOLD, ALISON LESLIE, (2001), *Memories of Anne Frank: Reflections of a Childhood Friend,* rebound by Sagebrush.

LEE, CAROL ANN, (1999), *Roses from the Earth: The Biography of Anne Frank,* London and New York: Viking Penguin.

LINDWER, WILLY, (1991), *The Last Seven Months of Anne Frank,* New York: Pantheon.

MOORE, BOB, (1997), *Victims and Survivors: The Nazi Persecution of the Jews in the Netherlands 1940-1945,* New York: St Martin's Press.

MULLER, MELISSA, (1999), *Anne Frank: The Biography,* London: Bloomsbury.

TAMES, RICHARD, (1998), *Anne Frank,* Oxford: Heinemann.

VAN DER ROL, RUND AND VERHOEVEN, RIAN, (1993), *Anne Frank: Beyond the Diary,* London and New York: Penguin Group.

# USEFUL WEBSITES

ANNE FRANK CENTRE USA, INC
www.annefrank.com

ANNE FRANK-FONDS
www.annefrank.ch

ANNE FRANK HOUSE
www.annefrank.org

ANNE FRANK TRUST UK
www.annefrank.org.uk

THE AUSCHWITZ-BIRKENAU STATE MUSEUM
www.auschwitz.org.pl

THE BERGEN-BELSON MEMORIAL
www.bergenbelsen.de/en

THE HOLOCAUST CENTRE, BETH SHALOM
www.bethshalom.com

HOLOCAUST EDUCATIONAL TRUST
www.het.org.uk

IMPERIAL WAR MUSEUM

www.iwm.org.uk

THE JEWISH MUSEUM

www.jewishmuseum.org.uk

UNITED STATES HOLOCAUST MEMORIAL MUSEUM

www.ushmm.org

YAD VASHEM

www.yadvashem.org

# INDEX